"When passion drives you, you are compelled to share it. I became a professional Certified Flight Instructor 22 years ago because I knew I had to share this incredible gift of flight that I had been given. Aviation continues to give back to those that give it away. To see and feel the aura of a student you have trained who has just soloed an airplane is an immeasurable gift to the instructor.

I met Jackie while attending a show where my wife and I advertise my flight school. She and her husband purchased a Discovery Flight on a whim to try it out. The flying bug bit Jackie hard. A few weeks later she called me, she had an epiphany, she was going to become a pilotina! She did. A mind and heart set on a path fueled by passion cannot be stopped. Now Jackie spreads aviation everywhere she goes. She understands how aviation can change lives. The passion for aviation is driving Jackie to plant seeds in others. In this book Jackie has assembled an incredible array of Latinas passionate about aviation. In their stories you will hear their passion and perhaps be inspired to start your journey into the amazing world of aviation."

—**David Spano,** Owner SimplyFLY flight school

"This is the perfect time for this book! What America needs right now is a jolt of dreamers reaching for the sky and getting there! The great Jacqueline Ruiz strokes hope and stokes dreams with Latinas in Aviation.

As a retired 30-year veteran of the Federal Aviation Administration, I lived to serve the courageous pilots who keep our world of aviation moving. Latinas of Aviation reveals the drive and determination of women who could not be discouraged in their personal journeys into the sky.

Ruiz has written a book about my favorite subjects; family and flying. Even if aviation slows in the coming years as the Covid-19 vaccine ends this pandemic, we are still going to be facing a pilot shortage. We are going to need more Latinas to strap on their headsets and advance the throttle to maximum forward thrust."

—**Robert James Allen, Sr.** Rochester, New York

Latinas in AVIATION

Stories of passion, power, and breaking into the aviation industry

JACQUELINE S. RUIZ

Latinas in AVIATION

This book is a compilation of stories from numerous people who have each contributed a chapter and is designed to provide inspiration to our readers. While the publisher and authors have used their best efforts in preparing this book by press time, they make no representations or warranties with respect to the accuracy or completeness of the contents within this book

It is sold with the understanding that the publisher and the individual authors are not engaged in the rendering of psychological, legal, accounting or other professional advice. The content and views in each chapter are the sole expression and opinion of its author and not necessarily the views of Fig Factor Media, LLC.

For more information, contact:

Jacqueline S. Ruiz
Fig Factor Media, LLC | www.figfactormedia.com

JJR Marketing, Inc. | www.jjrmarketing.com
Latinas in Aviation | www.latinasinaviation.com

Cover Design & Layout by Juan Pablo Ruiz
Printed in the United States of America

ISBN: 978-1-952779-22-0
Library of Congress Number: 2020943493

This book is dedicated to the young Latinas who dream of becoming pilots and leaders in the world of aviation. Dream high and touch the sky!

TABLE OF CONTENTS:

ACKNOWLEDGEMENTS

This book would not have taken off without the cooperation and support of so many people.

First of all, my husband, **Juan Pablo**, who supported me on my journey and surprised me with my first pair of aviation headphones. I also thank him for the creative direction of this book.

...and my children, **Guiliana and Leo**, who helped me through my training frustrations and rough landings with their gentle encouragement of, "It's ok, mom, you can try again tomorrow!"

Thank you to **David Spano** of SimplyFLY Flight School, for without your proximity, 40 years of experience, and passion for aviation, I may never have been inspired to take this journey and launch this book.

Thank you to my wonderful flight instructors, **Tony Sabos** and Peter Taylor, who helped me do more than I ever thought possible, and **Alan Zielinski**, who is not only an amazing FAA Examiner who gave me my license, but also a friend and supporter of my endeavors.

To all my **past, present, and future passengers**...including my Amelia teddy bear who accompanied me on my solo and has been with me on every flight...may we continue to soar high together!

Finally, I'd like to thank the editor, **Karen Dix**, who helped bring these stories to life, and **Gaby Hernández-Franch**, our tireless author concierge, and of course, all of the **authors in this book** who have willingly come forth to share their stories and had the bravery to jump into an industry where women, and especially Latinas, are so underrepresented. Your courage in the face of adversity and fear inspire me daily!

- **Jacqueline S. Ruiz**

INTRODUCTION

Dear Aviation,

I never planned for you to change my life, but that is what you have done!

When I walked into the flight school that summer day in 2015, it was as a marketing consultant to help SimplyFly increase their brand awareness. Then, I was offered the opportunity to take a discovery flight...and I felt the magnetic pull of your enchantment. I have been forever bewitched!

Nothing compares to the thrill of the ascent to the heavens or the heady view of a landscape that you provide. It sets my heart on fire!

The day I received my sports pilot's license I felt the excitement of being forever united with you. It was indeed one of my proudest achievements. Now, from my Instagram account to my custom-wrapped roadster, you have given me a new identity as the #pilotina—a name I am known by throughout the world!

But first, I discovered how so few women, and especially Latinas, know how wonderful you are. Only six percent of pilots are women, and of that small percentage, only about one percent are Latina pilots today in the United States.

Why should that be? These stories, told by those who love you as I do, show us the answer. The ladies within these pages have broken barriers, bucked tradition, and persevered through hardships and emotional, financial, and physical challenges to be with you, answering the call within their hearts. You beckoned them and they responded enthusiastically, despite the odds!

Just as I inspire Latina entrepreneurs with my successful book series, *"Today's Inspired Latina"*. I hope this unique anthology will change the lives of the authors within, as well as all who read their words.

Dear Aviation, this book is my thank you to you and the Latinas who pave the way to your glory, as well as those who long to feel your touch.

- Jacqueline S. Ruiz

EVELYN R. MIRALLES

Associate Vice President @ UHCL + Former NASA Chief Engineer + BBC 100 Women World + 2xCNET + Speaker + Consultant

Having the ability to fly and learn piloting skills are unique characteristics that began as, and have continued to be, mostly attributed to men. Yet as a young Latina woman, I had the prowess to study computing engineering and learn about aerospace at a time when few others were doing so.

Since then, I have devoted more than 27 years of my professional life learning and supporting human spaceflight exploration missions. My efforts culminated in training U.S. and international astronauts at NASA from 1992 to 2019 to perform the most dangerous task in the world, Spacewalking. Through focused work and determination, I had the privilege to pioneer the tools for virtual reality technology, helping prepare brave men and women to fly into space and accomplish seemingly impossible missions for the Space Shuttle and the International Space Station programs.

In time, it became obvious to me that the knowledge I had gained through years of work reflected only half of what my goals should be. Without giving back and inspiring others, I realized that my hard work and many hours of learning and perfecting all I knew could be literally lost in space.

It was during my journey to connect the 'knowledge with the giving' that I met the author of books such as *Today's Inspired Latina* and *Today's Inspired Young Latina*, Jacqueline Camacho-Ruiz, on a trip to New York City while supporting a Hispanic national event. Jacqueline's personality and obvious passion for aviation truly captured my attention and intrigued me to learn more. She is one of the few Latinas in the country who supports aspiring young female pilots and guides them to pursue their dreams within aviation. Such educational opportunities are extremely difficult to obtain at a young age, particularly without mentoring.

I was also impressed to learn that Jacqueline was about to embark on an historic air race which twenty women, including the famous Amelia Earhart, once flew across the United States over 91 years ago. These impressive qualities coupled with Jacqueline's own personal story and determination to give back, have prepared the way for this memorable book.

Latinas in Aviation is a collection of short stories, which are all celebrations of distinctive women in various roles within aviation, their stories told through accounts of their triumphs, their stumbles and their most crowning achievements. As you read, a fascinating discovery of true stories will unfold, from retired pilot veterans, to newly graduated pilots, aviation administrators, and military and civilian pilots – all with a unique passion for aviation endeavors and the impact they have on our world! The *storytellers* reveal their own experiences and inspirations, describing lives which set the stage for the next generation of Latinas who look to the sky with a dream.

I am humbled to write the preface for this special book, supporting Jacqueline's mission to encourage women to pursue careers in aviation. I believe that the aviation industry should continue to develop an awareness of the need for a more diverse workforce, and it should take decisive action to reach out to women. Aeronautics, aviation, and aerospace sciences are complex endeavors, with distinct components varying from design and engineering operations to management. Therefore, women desiring to have careers in these fields should have educational experiences in multiple disciplines in order to be fully prepared. For this reason, it is important to create a pipeline with varied female talent, to open up and provide the opportunity to gain experiences in multiple segments of the industry.

My mission while working at NASA was to enable men and women astronauts to travel to outer space, while inspiring exploration for all humankind. These incredible women pilots, who are highlighted so beautifully in this book, can be lauded for their courage and pioneering work. Their stories will aid in inspiring, today and in the future, millions of young women around the world to follow their dreams of flying high!

A SUCCESSFUL REBELLION

GRACIELA TISCAREÑO-SATO

CURRENT POSITION
Air Force Veteran, Bilingual Author & CEO of Gracefully
Global Group, LLC

FAVORITE AIRCRAFT
KC-135R Aerial Refueling Tanker

FAVORITE QUOTE
"On the other side of fear is the best version of yourself."

FUN FACT
I'm the author of the award-winning, bilingual *Captain Mama*
children's aviation book series – the first-ever book series in two
languages about women flying airplanes!

My parents Arturo and Tina were ambitious, hard-working
Mexican immigrants who arrived in the U.S. in the 1960s. My
father lived in Southern California first and worked as a tailor in

upscale men's clothing stores, dressing Hollywood stars for years. He met my mother in Ciudad Juarez on a trip home to visit his family; they married a few years later. I was born, just barely in the U.S., in a Catholic hospital in El Paso, Texas, just a quarter mile north of the border. After my birth, we spent a year in Arizona and then my father was offered a job at a new shopping mall in Greeley, Colorado. My parents bought a modest home in nearby Evans, had my four siblings, and faithfully provided for us.

THE REBEL RISES

We all spoke Spanish at home, a rule strictly enforced by my parents. My medium-sized agricultural community had very little diversity. As the oldest of five children, it felt natural to forge my own path through life. By eighth grade, my four best friends were white girls with college-educated parents. My mom would ask me, "Why you don't have any Mexican girlfriends?" I answered truthfully that I had very little in common with them.

My girlfriends shared my passionate interest in math and science, and were expected to attend college. They were either in the marching band, or volleyball or basketball teammates. My few Mexican-American peers smoked behind the school, flirted with boys, then disappeared after the final bell. My friends and athletic activity choices were not what Mami expected; she wanted me to be home helping her with childcare and household chores like the other girls in our neighborhood. She called me *"Rebelde!"* (Rebel!)

Instead, I was intrigued by musical and athletic

competitions, by my friends' bigger homes and private bedrooms, and their parents' careers (an educator, a transportation engineer, a helicopter pilot). As someone who spent summers road-tripping to El Paso and Ciudad Juarez, Mexico, in a car with six other people, I was especially jealous of my friends' family vacations to places like Hawaii and Austria. I wanted to pursue that type of globally-mobile lifestyle, despite my circumstances.

I understood the powerful influence of the traditional values associated with my Mexican and Catholic cultures – values which persist today with most immigrant families. While *saying* that an education was important, daughters were typically not raised to have aspirations beyond high school nor to move away from home to study. I was encouraged to accept the supposed limitations of our lower-middle-class status, find a nice man, marry and procreate.

Luckily, my mother Agustina had rebelled in her own way growing up in Mexico. She had finished high school, worked, and refused marriage until age twenty-six—a very rebellious act in mid-twentieth century Mexico! Mami was a big believer in education, although unable to pursue hers. One summer, she took us all to pick onions in the hot sun for two weeks, for very little pay. She wanted us to feel what life might be like without an education. I vowed to become a scholar and a professional.

To succeed I would need to rebel against cultural stereotypes, low educational expectations, and the often-heard message that I couldn't afford college. Mami said I could study but I would need to live at home, because a proper young woman didn't move out until she got married. I wish I was kidding.

I heard there were many college scholarships in the U.S., so I hung out at my counselor's office and asked Mrs. Burgess, "How does a student like me go to college?" I did what I advise young women to do today: I owned the process. Mrs. Burgess suggested I meet her husband, Air Force Major Burgess. Like most children of immigrants, I was clueless about military service in this country. I saw it as a diversion from college and avoided the recruiters in the school cafeteria. I knew nothing of the difference between enlisting after high school and completing a college degree first to become a commissioned officer. Major Burgess mentored me to apply for the four-year Air Force ROTC (Reserve Officer Training Corps) scholarship and my counselor helped me apply to my first-choice college, the University of California at Berkeley. I was accepted and awarded the four-year scholarship to study Architecture and Environmental Design.

After an eleven-hundred-mile road trip the following August, my family dropped me off at my dorm. This was the first time I saw my father cry. My drive to become a scholar at an elite university far from home, sight unseen, was shocking for my family. Yet my supportive parents didn't hold me back.

ADVENTURES IN THE AIR

Two years later, during the AFROTC summer career exploration program, I signed up for an orientation flight at a pilot training base in Phoenix. I was a roller coaster junkie and loved feeling strong G-forces, speed, and going upside-down.

Like most children of lower-middle-class immigrants however, I had never had the pleasure of riding in an airplane during childhood. Air Force Captain Dolly Delisa was my instructor pilot. When we took off in the T-37 jet trainer, I felt exhilarated. She gave me the controls and taught me to do aileron rolls. I loved the adrenaline rush and speed! Captain Delisa asked about my academic major as she observed my interest and aptitude for learning to fly. I shared that I was studying architecture and would serve in a civil engineering unit to repay my four years of service for accepting the scholarship. I thought I was locked into that career choice. She told me I wasn't locked into anything. She could see in my eyes that I belonged in the air.

"Go back and tell the ROTC staff you want to fly," she advised. "There is a board selection process and I think you can get a pilot or a navigator training slot. Go for it!"

I followed my airborne mentor's advice when I returned to Berkeley and the staff placed me into the selection process for officers with aeronautical ratings. These are the silver aviator wings on the Air Force blue uniform. Months later, I was selected to attend flight school upon graduation. Thank God for that woman aviator's inspiration!

Because of that experience, I tell young women to do whatever it takes to get to college. College teaches you how to learn and to learn new things. Most importantly, it puts you where amazing opportunities can surface. Then you can choose to walk through interesting doors as you discover new curiosities. Would any of these aviation moments have happened if I had stayed in my small town to work after high school?

I entered the active duty Air Force as a Second Lieutenant and Undergraduate Navigator Training student at Mather Air Force Base in Sacramento six months after graduating from Cal. I had completed all academic courses for my degree plus the aerospace studies required for AFROTC cadets to become commissioned officers. I was the only woman in my UNT class and graduated in the top fifth.

On assignment night, I selected the KC-135R refueling tanker, which I describe as a flying gas station. My family was present at my UNT graduation ceremony. They saw my fellow Cal band trombonist, Genro Sato, pin my silver wings to my uniform; he became my fiancée later that day when he proposed at the Officers Club.

From there, I moved to Castle AFB to receive specialized training with three other people–a pilot, copilot, and boom operator–to learn how to operate the KC-135R and conduct aerial refueling missions. It was wild! My job in the flight deck was to do the math and direct our flying gas station to rendezvous with other airplanes at an exact location and time anywhere on the planet. It was amazing to have an airplane fly up behind us and attach to our "boom" – the long pipe that transfers fuel from our ten fuel tanks to theirs. I have many photos of that awesome sight taken from the back window (the boom pod).

Three months after marrying Genro at San Francisco's Treasure Island, I deployed to Riyadh, Saudi Arabia for Operation Southern Watch to help enforce the Southern No-Fly

Zone over Iraq after the end of Operation Desert Storm. We flew refueling sorties for combat air patrols over Baghdad, preventing Saddam Hussein from targeting civilians. My crew was awarded the prestigious Air Medal for meritorious achievement in combat flight operations. This happened ten months *before* Congress lifted the Combat Exclusion Law that supposedly barred women from assignment to combat aircraft and operations, where we'd been unofficially serving for years. I was one of many women in the military who fought for this change so women could serve (and lead) in all roles for which they qualify. I'm thrilled that many women aviators have since served in combat aircraft and subsequently in senior leadership roles.

NEW MISSIONS

During my decade in service, I visited over a dozen nations, flew thousands of hours, and taught students in the classroom and in the air. I ran a NATO airlift control center in Italy and a counter-narcotics operations support center in Ecuador. During the latter, I researched and wrote my master thesis to complete my graduate degree in international management from Whitworth University in Spokane, Washington where I was stationed.

I then left the military to work as a global technology marketing manager in Silicon Valley. Now that I was no longer deploying, Genro and I decided to start our family. In 2010, as the mother of three young children, I founded Gracefully Global Group LLC, an educational publishing, digital content, and multicultural marketing firm. We creatively serve the

K-12 education market, universities, and corporations with inspirational literature, workshops, and keynote presentations in two languages. I've designed workshops, online courses, and a marketing guidebook to help transitioning military servicemembers craft their AUTHENTIC Personal Branding BEFORE writing resumes or online profiles.

We published the award-winning, bilingual Captain Mama children's book series to share my personal story. *Good Night Captain Mama* was inspired by my son, Kiyoshi, the night before a Veterans Day preschool visit. He spotted me in my flight suit on his way to bed, was curious about my "costume" and patches, and called me "Captain Mama." The second book is Captain Mama's Surprise – a fascinating field trip to the airplane where Captain Mama works, narrated by her son. We're developing the third book in this unique aviation series which teaches children why mommies choose to wear military uniforms and to fly jets. The series has won six literary awards in international competitions, and the Obama Administration recognized my work with White House "Champion of Change, Woman Veteran Leader" honors.

My mission now? To raise educational expectations for Latino American students and inspire children, especially girls, to pursue well-paying, technical careers like aviation. I tell my aviation service story this way to show students that neither the sky, nor birth circumstances, need to limit what we can achieve.

As Genro and I raise our three teens, I actively mentor young adults. For middle and high school students, I published *Latinnovating: Green American Jobs and the Latinos Creating*

Them, the first book in a planned series showcasing the positive contributions of Latino innovation leaders in emerging green economy industries. *Latinnovating* opens students' eyes to academic majors and careers while promoting entrepreneurship and sustainability.

I've always believed that on the other side of fear is the best version of yourself, a message I deliver coast-to-coast as a bilingual keynote speaker. I advocate a gospel of rebellion against low expectations, gender stereotypes, and naysayers of higher education. This mindset helped me exceed my childhood dreams to travel and to enjoy a globally-mobile lifestyle. I bet it'll work for you to achieve whatever you've imagined for yourself. Aim High!

Graciela Tiscareño-Sato is a U.S. Air Force veteran, award-winning author/speaker and CEO of Gracefully Global Group, LLC, an educational publishing, digital content, and multicultural marketing firm. She can be reached at (510) 542-9449, through GracefullyGlobal.com, and on social media networks LinkedIn and Instagram by searching her full name.

COVID-19 POSTSCRIPT

It's a fascinating coincidence that the last conference I attended before WHO declared the pandemic was the Women in Aviation International Conference in Orlando, held during the first week of March. I networked with more than five thousand, like-minded sisters and allies from around the world, and signed copies of my *Captain Mama* children's books! I finally met my SHEro, Major General Jeannie Leavitt, currently the Commander of U.S. Air Force Recruiting Service, who was the first woman assigned a combat aircraft in 1993, just after the Combat Exclusion Law was lifted! I attended the Women Military Aviators Flight Suit Social and reconnected with astronaut Eileen Collins, KC-135R pilot Colonel Kelly Hamilton, and *mi amiga* USAF Lt. Col. Olga Custodio, the first Latina to complete Air Force pilot training! I met Latinas in various, fascinating aviation careers.

When I returned home, Genro and I transitioned to teleworking and homeschooling three teenagers. They adapted nicely, although my oldest child, who is blind, needs more assistance since she learns best by reading Braille and by touch – not by listening to voices on the computer. We are fine, but I try not to think about the revenue I lost from the cancellation of public speaking events and associated product sales through early fall.

I'm now delivering my *AUTHENTIC Personal Branding* workshops and *Captain Mama* author visits virtually. I'm blessed; I was already using a virtual service delivery model and have kept my business alive! I'm also grateful for the additional family time – we've played more games, eaten more meals on the deck together, and gone on more bike rides than in past years. We planted our garden early and finished the deck!

Even if this novel coronavirus erases the rest of my conferences in 2020, I'm so glad I didn't miss WIA and the opportunity to spend four days with women who love flying!

MY FLYING STORY

OLGA ESTHER NEVAREZ CUSTODIO

CURRENT POSITION

Lieutenant Colonel, USAFR, Retired

Captain, American Airlines, Retired

FAVORITE AIRCRAFT

The T-38. I was the first Latina woman to fly it.

FAVORITE QUOTE

"Querer es Poder."

"Where there is a will, there is power."

FUN FACT

I recently appeared in a Modelo beer commercial.

Our defining moments in life are tests for us to see who we are and what we are able to do. Your experiences up to that moment are what will help define you. I know this through firsthand experience.

"So, there I was," I say, as most pilots do as they start their flying stories...

It was a warm, west Texas day. The tower cleared me for takeoff. Taking the runway, I looked down final to make sure there wasn't an aircraft on approach and proceeded to lower and lock the canopy. Lined up on the centerline, holding brakes, I pushed the throttles to full power. Engine instruments checked. I released the brakes and started rolling down the runway.

V1, check engine instruments, V2, rotate, and liftoff. Gear and flaps up, cross-check, and then BAM! The windscreen goes dark...

Everything I had experienced and learned about life and myself brought me to this moment, and I was going to need all of it.

Successful people usually start their journey with a dream, desire, or goal, whether it was as early as elementary school or just yesterday. I always say, "It's never too late."

MILITARY MEMORIES

If you had met me when I was younger, you would never guess I would have the experiences and achieve the goals that I have. I was very shy, quiet, and insecure.

I was born in San Juan, Puerto Rico, but only spent my first three months on the island before my mom and I left to join my father, who was a career army soldier. Growing up an Army brat, my father was my best role model of sacrifice, service, and love of country. He served 23 years in the U.S. Army. Serving during World War II and the Korean War at a very young age, he was finally recognized for his service a few years ago. Congress awarded the 65th Infantry Regiment, the only all-Hispanic regiment in U.S. military history, known as the "Borinqueneers," the Congressional Gold Medal of Honor in 2014. Their valor and service, second to none, was an exemplary demonstration of sacrifice and dedication.

We lived in many different states and countries around the world, moving every two to three years. Attending new schools and making new friends every time was not easy. My parents would tell me that it wasn't forever, and we made the best of where we lived. They also showed me how to be proud of my Puerto Rican heritage, and we spoke Spanish at home. Living in Asia, the Middle East, and South America taught me to appreciate our democracy and all the opportunities we have living in the United States. It also taught me to respect different cultures and their people.

I knew that I wanted to follow in my father's footsteps and enter military service. I didn't know what my military service would be, but I knew I was committed to the journey. I could never have imagined I would become the First Latina U.S. military pilot and first Latina American Airlines pilot.

It took me ten years to finally get the opportunity to serve in the U.S. Air Force. When I was 16 years old and in my first year at the University of Puerto Rico, they denied me the opportunity to enter Reserves Officer Training Corps (ROTC) and be commissioned as a U.S. Air Force officer.

Incredibly, it wasn't till years later that I realized it was discrimination. The ROTC Commander brushed me off, making me think I had not passed an exam. He pulled it out of a drawer without making me fill out any formal application or documentation. Because I was young and naive, I respected authority and believed him. Women were first allowed into the ROTC program a year after my attempt, but I had left with the thought that I had not passed the exam. I wonder how I would have felt if the Commander had let me know that women weren't allowed, versus making me believe I had not passed. But that experience did not make me give up my desire to serve.

EARNING MY WINGS

Opportunity came when I turned 26 years of age and was already a wife and mother with a promising Department of Defense job. The U.S. Air Force had finally opened the pilot career field to women, and they were recruiting. I have felt comfortable in airplanes since I had first flown to the U.S. at three months old and spent much time crisscrossing the world as I moved around with my parents. I realized my desire to serve had never faded, and now I had been given the most significant opportunity to serve my country with the biggest challenge. The journey was full of barriers and challenges, and without role models, it was even harder.

Now back to my flying story.

...Looking up to the windscreen now covered with blood

and feathers, I immediately went into emergency mode. The first steps in any flight emergency are to maintain aircraft control, analyze the situation, and take the appropriate action. In my T-37 aircraft, during the first phase of Air Force undergraduate pilot training on a solo flight, my pilot skills, situational awareness, and mental attitude was being put to the test.

This defining moment, in which I successfully handled the emergency and safely landed the aircraft, gave me the confidence to know that I had what it took to be a pilot. In this profession, you must have some skills to become successful, but motivation, combined with those skills, is a huge part of reaching success. Later, as an instructor pilot I would see this in my students.

Ultimately, I learned to navigate the challenges and barriers and became the best pilot I could be. I graduated in the top five percent of my U.S. Air Force Undergraduate Pilot training class and was the only female as well. This distinction allowed me to get my fighter qualification to fly the T-38 aircraft, a supersonic ejection seat aircraft, as an instructor pilot. The fighter designation of this aircraft was the F-5. It was the fastest, badass aircraft that women could fly in the U.S. Air Force inventory at the time. It was the aircraft flown by the U.S. Air Force Thunderbirds Flight Demonstration Team. But the law did not allow women in combat, so fighter aircraft were not available for women. Thirteen years later, the law changed. We had proven that we had what it took to fly and are now allowed to show that we could engage in combat.

BREAKING BARRIERS

I love the experience of flight and being at the controls. I see the world from a different perspective and know that I am part of something so much bigger than myself. I know that my faith, the support of family, friends, and mentors (which I had to seek out) were an essential part of my success.

When I entered the aviation career field, women made up only .01 percent of pilots in the military and commercial airlines. As for Latinas in aviation, you might have been able to count them with one hand, if that. To date, women pilots have risen to only a seven percent representation in the pilot profession in the last 40 years.

Navigating through the challenges and barriers in this male-dominated profession was not an easy task, but I knew I was in it for the long term. I believe women are equally capable as men in all fields, especially aviation. With the right amount of encouragement, support, representation, and funding, we can elevate these numbers—and make women be known and respected in a field still dominated by men.

I am proud of my success in fulfilling my dream of serving my country and becoming a pilot, without knowing any female who had ever dared to do so. I made American history as the first Latina Air Force and American Airlines pilot.

Becoming the first women pilot in several U.S. Air Force flying positions and the first Latina, too, was not my purpose nor my motivation. My over-30 years of combined experience in military and civilian aviation and over 11,000 flight hours serves me well. I am a dedicated STEM advocate, motivational speaker, and mentor. Serving on the board and working with several aviation nonprofit organizations, I support the vision and mission of getting more women in aviation, especially Latinas and women from underserved communities.

I am dedicated in everything that I do and in anything that I set out to accomplish. But I did not do it alone and worked hard in having a work and life balance. I thank my husband, Edwin, children, Marcia, and Edwin II and my parents for their love, help, and continued support in my endeavors. Their sacrifices allowed me to succeed.

My life's mantra is *"Querer es Poder,"* which I translate as "Where there is a will, there is power." I challenge you to continue to define your dream and allow yourself to see your potential to fulfill your purpose.

Olga is a retired USAFR Lieutenant Colonel and American Airlines Captain who addresses audiences around the country. She is currently working on her memoirs and can be contacted at www. purflygirl.com.

COVID-19 POSTSCRIPT

Coping with the COVID-19 pandemic started after my return from a Spring Break trip with my family in mid-March. I had just attended an international aviation conference and visited the Disney and Universal Parks with my grandson and family. We knew we had to self-quarantine for two weeks and decided to be together. We did not get any symptoms during that time, but the stay-at-home order came before our two weeks had passed.

Now, we continue working from home and attending school virtually, with the dining room a part-time office, and the bedroom as a part-time school. The living room and back yard are a makeshift respite to escape "work" and "school," and the kitchen is a "masterclass," changing our titles from cooks to chefs. Priorities are redefined, and we are very conscious of "need" versus "want."

I live near the airport's flight path, and when I sit on my patio I watch the arrivals or departures, depending on the wind direction. My thoughts are on the flight crews and how they are coping. Air traffic is light, with more private jets than airliners. I ponder on, remembering my return to flying after 9/11 and wondering if it is the same for pilots now. I reminisce about past vacation travels and imagine a not-so-distant future, traveling in a different and changing world.

As I write this, it is day fifty-four of staying safe at home. I am grateful we are comfortable with each other and get along. However, I am most thankful that all my family is safe and healthy. It's all I can ask and hope for right now. We are strong, resilient, and I know we will survive this because we have hope.

FLYING FOR DAD

JACQUELINE PULIDO

CURRENT POSITION
Flight Instructor & Airbus 320 Captain

FAVORITE AIRCRAFT
Airbus 320. The more you fly it the more you love it.

FAVORITE QUOTE
"If God is your copilot, switch seats."
"The Lord will guide you always." Isaiah 58:11

FUN FACT
I was the first woman pilot at Volaris Airlines.

When my sisters and I were little, we would set up our dining room chairs in a row, one in front of the other, to resemble the seat configuration in a commercial airliner. This was our "plane" and we were the flight crew. If I was playing "dad" that day, I would stand by the cockpit like a pilot, and welcome imaginary passengers onto the "aircraft." Meanwhile, my sister, who would be playing mom, was a flight attendant, helping our "passengers" find their seats. Then, she would begin the pre-take-off and safety announcements. We all knew those announcements by heart, and could recite them in our high, sweet voices because we had flown so often with our parents. Then, when we were ready for "take-off," I would sit down in the "cockpit," make the necessary announcements to the cabin, and we would be on our way to some fanciful place. Soon after, snack and beverage service would begin.

With childhood games like that, I guess you can see how much of an aviation family we were!

THE FLYING FAMILY

My mom and dad met while working on a commercial airliner with Mexicana Airlines. They fell in love, got married, and had three beautiful daughters who they raised in Toluca, Mexico. My mother stopped flying as a flight attendant to stay home with us, but she made sure we fell in love with aviation, just as she and my dad had. I have so many memories as a child of seeing my Dad in his pilot's uniform, getting ready for work. Many, many times, he took all of us with him when he had longer flights or a three or four-day layover. We were just babies, but I remember flying to wonderful vacation spots like Chicago, Cancun, Puerto Vallarta, and Los Angeles.

Mom always made the trip fun, engaging us by talking about the plane and explaining what was going on in each phase of the flight. We could even visit my Dad in the cockpit and he would explain all the fascinating switches, gadgets, radars and screens. All three of us were amazed by his work and really admired my dad for what he did.

As we grew older, we could fly alone with dad too. We would visit our grandparents in Chicago. Flying just became part of our way of life.

I was in elementary school when I started telling my dad I wanted to become a pilot just like him. My dream was for us to fly together, with him at the controls as pilot, and me as his co-pilot.

Then, when I was 14 years old, my dad started to get sick. For a long time they couldn't figure out what was wrong with him, and then he got the diagnosis. It was a brain tumor. The news devastated us all. The tumor was operable, but we knew that it would end my dad's flying career. I also knew it was the end of my dream to be his co-pilot. However, it wasn't the end of my dream to be a pilot. He came through the surgery and started treatment, and we did our best to keep his spirits high.

When I was 17, my parents sat me down and asked me if I was serious about becoming a pilot. My dad was no longer working, and money was tight, but I told them it was something I really wanted to do and I would give my all to make it happen. They vowed to support me through it. So, my mom had to start working to support our family, and we will be forever grateful.

In the U.S., smaller airports are plentiful and can usually be found within miles, but from our hometown, the nearest one with a flight school was in Cuernavaca, a two-hour drive from Toluca. On weekends, we would make it a family outing. My family would relax and picnic while I got my two or three hours of flying in at the airport. Sometimes my grandparents would come to watch. They even helped finance my flight training.

When I finally got my pilot's license, it was a bittersweet day when I was able to take my dad up in a Cessna for a flight. I had always wanted to be his First Officer, and now he was mine, but when he took the controls, he flew like an angel. I was impressed and amazed when he told me he had not been at the controls of such a small airplane in more than twenty years! He flew it like it was a daily ritual. I knew I wanted to fly with him even more, and I wanted to figure out a way to do that.

RALLY DAYS

Opportunity came in 2001 when I heard about an international ladies cup taking place overseas in the Netherlands. It sounded really exciting to me, so I began asking around and putting together a women's team. The entry fee and cost to participate was high so my mother and I began looking for sponsors. My mom was, and still is, my biggest supporter. She helped me write letters and drove me everywhere to ask for help. I can still hear her voice cheering for me in everything I do. My aviation school helped out supporting us too, as did my grammar school, my grandparent's business, the pilot's union and the Mexican division of Shell Aviation services.

To compete and qualify as a women's team, a woman had

to be captain of the aircraft. Males could be on board but could not be in command. My entire family, including dad, flew in a day early to get familiar with the plane, air space and airport. I was only 19 at the time and so excited and humbled by the whole experience. I only saw one other girl my age there, but I was very impressed by the mothers, grandmothers, and young adult women that I met. Most were commercial airline pilots that flew for KLM or in the military. In other words, really tough competition!

The route was an exciting, two-day, cross-country route across a terrain completely different than Mexico. Handicaps were given for the limits of the airplane, such as speed and size, and then there were checkpoints along the way that each had time limits. Points were awarded for various aviation elements such as time, altitude, and efficiency. Even though we had done our best to fundraise, I remember we ran out of money on the way back from the race and had to spend the night at the airport before heading back home. It was all part of the experience!

During the race, dad sat in the back, along with my flight instructors who came as teammates. Once in the air, I was amazed at the beautiful, lush, green terrain so different from home. It was not unlike a scavenger hunt as I had to find certain landmarks along the route as I flew, and dad and the team helped spot them from fifteen hundred feet. I was used to radio communication in Spanish, but now I had to attune my ear to English with a Dutch accent. I was required to land on shorter runways than I had ever experienced before. Everything seemed like new and I could feel myself becoming a better pilot for having the experience.

At the conclusion of the race, they held a special, formal gala to announce the winners. We were the only Latinos there and everyone was so welcoming; they had even invited the Mexican ambassador on our behalf! There were many trophies given out and our team was thrilled to be honored for range and endurance competition. The winner took home a beautiful Breitling ladies' watch as a prize.

My dad was so proud of me and I was so proud he could be with me on the race, acting as a kind of spiritual co-pilot for me. It wouldn't be my last competition. I competed again in 2003 and 2005, with different crews. We didn't always win but we sure had fun. My whole family was with me during those races too. They always have my back.

Aside from racing, I completed flight school and started on my journey to become a commercial pilot. I hit some speedbumps. I was a ground instructor in 2001 when aviation was halted in Mexico after 9/11. So I moved to flying corporate jets to get my hours, but I also needed scholarship money to continue moving forward. I needed a type rating and more experience too.

SPECIAL FIRSTS

Then I started reading about the Ninety-Nines. The Ninety-Nines is a non-profit, international organization of licensed women pilots from forty-four countries. I knew they had some scholarship opportunities for me, so I approached them, asking if they had a chapter nearby. They told me they did not, then asked,

"Would you like to start one?"

I gathered my women pilot friends and asked them to help get the chapter off the ground. I became the Governor of the Mexican Chapter. It ended up being quite complicated, and we needed to look for sponsors so we could offer programs for women pilots. We were successful in launching an essay contest to win a Lear Jet 25 rating training. But only two pilots submitted the essay, and one of them was me. We continued to build a Ninety-Nine's chapter near my hometown.

When it came time for me and my fellow women pilots to begin applying to the local airlines, nobody seemed to be having much luck. Finally, in 2004, I joined Aerounion, a cargo airline and flew a beautiful A-300 B4. I never imagined my first opportunity in an airline would be "flying a heavy." Later, in 2005, I was hired by a new airline called Volaris. They had brand new A319's and a promising future. My prayers were answered and I could see myself building the rest of my career with them. I was the first woman pilot ever hired at the airline!

I recognized the heavy responsibility right away. I was opening up doors for other female pilots so I was nervous about doing everything correctly. I did not want to shut the doors for anybody. I was already used to an all-male environment from my other aviation jobs, so the biggest adjustment was finding a balance in my relationship with them. I was only 23 years old, so most of the time they would treat me like a daughter, even asking me to leave the room if the conversation was getting too "male." Five years later, I was upgraded to captain. Eventually, the flight crew and I formed a family and I was with the airline for 11 years. Volaris was a great place for a woman pilot like me.

I stopped flying in 2016 to give birth to my son, Mateo. I do miss flying, but for me and my husband, who is also a A320 flight instructor for Vivaaerobus, our priority is our little one.

To scratch my aviation itch, I took a position as a flight safety officer at Vivaaerobus, from 2017-19, where I was responsible for Flight Operational Quality Assurance (FOQA) analysis and risk mitigation focused on safety and pilots. I helped pilots improve their safety measures and processes, and it was a very enriching and fulfilling experience. Currently, I'm back to work as an A320 simulator instructor, doing training with the next generation of pilots and sharing my experience. I miss flying but know I will be back again.

In the meantime, I'm happy to see that the airline that hired me as their first woman now has about 36 women pilots on their team. In my work as an instructor, I'm proud to be preparing women to enter the field that seemed reserved for men.

I'm happy to say my dad, who is my inspiration for everything I do in aviation, is still with us. I'm so proud that I could follow in his footsteps and become a commercial airline pilot. I'm even more proud that I can inspire others, just as he has inspired me, to think about careers in aviation.

Jacqueline Pulido is a former captain at Volaris Airlines and a current simulator instructor of the Airbus 320. She can be reached at Jackpu26@hotmail.com.

COVID-19 POSTSCRIPT

I was concerned when I started reading about how COVID-19 was affecting other countries but never thought it would affect our lives this way. We were in New York on March 19, 2020 getting ready for takeoff, and we were feeling anxious to get home ASAP. There's no place like home during times like these. I felt like we were in a movie when we were in the airport security check line surrounded by many people already wearing face masks and just being silent.

This pandemic has definitely taught me and my family many things. The biggest one is to trust that God will never leave us or forsake us. It's gotten pretty scary and our faith is holding us together. The other thing is that there is nothing more important than being healthy and together.

A huge part of our life is on hold. Our jobs are on hold, our pay has been affected, and our lives are forever changed. We are blessed to be able to stay at home together, to have enough food, water, and to cover our basic needs. We are connected with our friends and family much more than ever. We are happy to see the sky cleaner and nature just being able to recover a bit from our damage. We pray we can all learn from this terrible situation and when things return to normal we can be more human.

YOUNG, BUT IN CHARGE!

ANDREA PALACIOS

CURRENT POSITION
Captain Embraer 190, Conviasa Airlines

FAVORITE AIRCRAFT
The Embraer 190. It's my home away from home!

FAVORITE QUOTE
"It is necessary to love to fly." -Amelia Earhart.

FUN FACT
I can't stand insects and as a child, a scorpion stung me at a hotel in Orlando-Florida.

It was a typical flight in Venezuela on my Embraer 190, for Conviasa Airlines. I was standing at the cockpit door with the other crew members, greeting the passengers as they climbed aboard. I was 22 years old and already serving as a co-pilot on the commercial flight. A man entered the plane and looked at me in a funny way as he glanced at my uniform.

"You're going to be the pilot?!" he asked me, with shock and surprise in his voice.

"Yes, I am," I replied, holding back my smile. "Good morning!"

"No, no, no, I do not believe you," he continued. "You can really fly this thing?"

I just nodded and smiled as he walked away and took his seat. By now, I'm used to it. Every passenger who boards must give you their confidence and trust. Being a woman pilot is a big enough surprise, yet alone being under the age of 30.

After the flight, he came over to speak to me, apologized for his initial reaction and said he was just so shocked because he had never seen a woman fly a plane. He congratulated me on reaching my goal and I could tell that he now believed not only in me, but in any other woman pilot he would meet from then on.

Most passengers are used to seeing middle-aged men at the controls of their plane. Instead they get me, the tenacious girl who earned her commercial pilot's license and became the youngest female commercial pilot in Latin America!

ROOTS OF AVIATION

The Palacios have been an "aviation family" for generations. Almost all of my family members do something with aviation. My dad was a fighter pilot in the Venezuelan Air Force before becoming a commercial pilot, and my mother also served in the Air Force. My sister and aunts are flight attendants, and I have many other relatives who have careers as aviation engineers, flight dispatchers, and airport security. Maybe aviation is in our blood!

I'm the oldest of five children, including three sisters and two brothers. However, it was my father who inspired my journey. I remember my first flight with him. I was seven years old. We got in his plane and he told me we were going to take off. He let me feel the commands as we headed down the runway and I remember being so excited as the plane gathered speed, then started to lift higher and higher off the ground. I had that "butterflies in your stomach" feeling that is a lot like being in love for the first time.

When I was 17, I went with my father to an airline where he worked. There, I found a new appreciation for the airlines. My father was the director of operations then, and my mom was the director of air accident investigation in Venezuela. I was then mature enough at that age to understand the workings of the industry, the role of the commercial airline pilot, and everything I had seen as a child. I had a chance to visit the cockpit, too, and experience the responsibility and stress of being a real pilot. I was convinced! When I graduated high school in 2009, I entered a special civil aviation school called CIAC Miguel Rodriguez. There were three women and seventeen men, and we flew aircraft like Cessna 150 and 182RG. I did well there, and even received a scholarship.

I was lucky to have the support of my parents who gave me such a great example in my life. "You can be whatever you want to be," they would tell me. My goal was to become captain of a commercial airliner and according to a Venezuela aeronautical regulation 60, that meant 1,500 flight hours and being over the age of 21 years old. In 2012, I graduated with my commercial pilot's license, and was delighted when I was hired by Consorcio Venezolano de Industrias Aeronauticas y Servicios Aereos (Conviasa), Venezuela's largest airline.

THE EMBRAER

I was lucky because at that time, the president of the airline was General Cesar Martínez, who wanted to train younger people on the newer generation of more technologically advanced airplanes. The airline had recently purchased fifteen Embraer 190 aircraft. General Martinez had confidence in me and the others in my training class. I was the only woman in a class of 17 men who trained on the Embraer, and in May of 2013, we were sent to St. Louis, Missouri for simulator training. There, I trained as a first officer, practicing all possible emergencies that can occur on a real flight. At the end of our training, we were evaluated by an inspector from the INAC (National Institute of Civil Aviation Venezuela).

I like to joke that the Embraer 190 is too easy to learn to fly, or at least it was for me, because it is so modern, it is like one giant computer. Conviasa is the only airline in Venezuela to fly the Embraer 190. The flight models have 104 seats for passengers and five seats for the flight crew, not counting the two additional seats for the pilots. For passengers, it has two rows of two seats on each side, divided by the aisle to access them.

As expected, the project to train young pilots was a success, and my colleagues and I passed all tests. A year later, I was a first officer (co-pilot) and I began my intense training as a pilot. I felt very lucky to learn from the experienced pilots at Conviasa and they were great mentors who willingly shared their knowledge with all of us.

I fly for an airline that is very much a product of the person in charge, and as the only woman on the Embraer 190 team, I've also always felt the pressure to perform well. But I've been prepared to do that by my training, which has been very rigorous and demanding. When the airline changed presidents, I suddenly found I was no longer being considered for promotions. Even though I was completely qualified by my age and hours of flight time, I was often passed over. When I asked why, I was even on occasion given the reason that I was just "too young," even though I was well over 21, the minimum age of a captain.

At first, I was angry and frustrated by the reality that I was not being valued for all I could do. It was hard enough trying to get ahead in a male-dominated industry as a woman, but to be young as well really made it difficult. So many of my bosses believed that young people weren't mature or just didn't know enough to be in such an important position. Between my age and my gender, I need to prove myself and my worthiness to sit in the cockpit every day of my career.

But I wasn't about to give up on wanting to become captain. Others in my life began encouraging me to finish my university studies, which I had started working on during my flight training.

That way, if I never reached my goal of captain, I would at least finish my degree in international business. So, I studied, and I flew, looking forward to a promotion that I knew would come someday.

My bosses did not understand why I wanted to study something else. Sometimes, because of my flights, I did not have the time to study for my school exams. At the same time, I was expected to keep up on any updates on the plane and always be reviewing procedures. During that period of time, I remember I never was able to take a vacation because I was either studying, watching classes, taking exams, or flying in a simulator. I intensified my studies by taking classes in summers and during holiday breaks. My goal was to graduate in four years, and I didn't know if I would actually make it!

WEARING CAPTAIN'S WINGS

In 2018, our airline got a new president again by the name of General Ramon Velasquez Araguayan. He believes in the development of women and was firmly interested in my promotion. I do think because I was studying for something else, my bosses may have felt I was not fully committed to my aviation career, and that may have halted my ascent to captain. Or, it could have just been the culture of "machismo" in the aeronautical field and the difficulty of men accepting women into the industry. Either way, thank God that the new president did not see it that way. He supported me in my studies, and I was so excited that after six years and 3,000 hours of flight time, I received the promotion to Captain at the age of 27! In 2019, I completed my degree in international trade, in four years, just as I hoped I would! So, I now have that as an alternative career possibility if ever I want to leave the airlines.

Conviasa now has three female pilots, including two first officers and me as the only captain. I'm so glad to see that other women are now pursuing their dreams and willing to overcome the obstacles that we face in a male-dominated industry. Meanwhile, I continue enjoying my life as a pilot and my view from the cockpit of the plane, or as I call it "the best office in the world!" I typically fly between 70-90 hours a month and enjoy the diversity in my work. Between the people, the weather, and the routes, every day is different. I also enjoy leading my crew in communication and briefings and I emphasize my openness to any doubt or discomfort any of my crew members may have with me. I try to be understanding so that they know me as someone they can trust who can slowly break down the barriers that older people often have with young people, or men have with women. If they see me in command, doing my job well, they will be just like the male passengers who are shocked by my presence when they board the plane. They will get to know and trust me through my work.

It's amazing to know that I have made my dream of becoming a commercial airline pilot come true, and that my accomplishment has helped advance women in the world of aviation in my country. I also appreciate changing the minds of those who board the plane and see a woman pilot! Latinas are a hardworking, determined sort and that can achieve success in aviation, or any other field they pursue. We all can do our part by reaching our goals and breaking down the paradigms of what we are "supposed" to do and what we can achieve. We can surprise them all.

Andrea Palacios is Captain of the Embraer 190 aircraft for Conviasa Airlines in Venezuela. She can be reached at Instagram @ andre_p1 or on Twitter @andree_p1.

COVID-19 POSTSCRIPT

COVID-19 was devastating news for the aviation industry and for me as well. My work hours have decreased considerably. I used to fly between 60 and 95 hours a month and now only do a maximum of 10 hours due to the decrease in flights. The protocol at the airport and how we board flights has changed, as well as the briefing we give to our crew, from wearing gloves and masks with protective suits to getting tested for COVID-19 after each humanitarian flight.

There have been many cases that have affected my professional and personal life. It is also stressful for pilots not to be able to fly. Letting go of that adrenaline rush we get from taking off in a plane is very sad. But I hope and wish this situation ends in a positive way for everyone and that my beloved aviation industry can bounce back better than ever.

JESSIKA HERNÁNDEZ

CURRENT POSITION
Flight Instructor at JW Aviation

FAVORITE AIRCRAFT
Tie between the Boeing 747 and the F-18 "Super Hornet"

FAVORITE QUOTE
"Life is too short to choose anything that doesn't light a fire inside of you."

FUN FACT
My friends say that I love my milk with a splash of coffee and as a Colombian, I probably should be better at my coffee etiquette.

I knew I was destined to become a pilot. I just never knew it would be in the United States!

I was born and raised in Colombia and basically grew up on a Colombian Air Force base. Both of my parents served in the

Air Force and are still active duty today. My mother had a civilian job and my father was not a pilot, but he handled logistics and support for troop deployment.

THE LOVE OF FLYING

I grew up surrounded by the military and the cool, breathtaking aircraft we used to defend the country. I routinely witnessed the training and live firing exercises, which are very scary and strange to see for non-military people, but I always thought were very interesting. For me, though, the military aircraft were the most exciting part of living on the base.

I savored the opportunities I had to see the aircraft up close. My father worked at the end of a secure ramp that led right up to the planes. Sometimes, on special occasions, I could get onto the ramp, walk right up to the planes and helicopters and get a chance to peek in at all the intriguing levers, dials, and buttons. It was like I was getting an inside glimpse into the secret life of a military pilot. I was fascinated by all the planes that came through the base and watching the aircraft and helicopters take off was an amazing experience that never got old.

There were also events like "Soldier for a Day" in which I was able to get a close-up encounter with the airplanes and helicopters, and sometimes there were airshows where my friends and I could also get a chance to sit in the cockpit and pretend to be fighters. Some of our family friends were pilots and they showed me some of the planes they flew at the time too.

Seeing a military aircraft, though, was nothing compared

to flying in a military aircraft! It is fairly easy to catch a ride in a military transport plane in Colombia if you are part of the immediate family of someone who works on the base. I was lucky to have the chance to travel for vacations and to visit my parents from college on some of the airplanes. Being in one of those high-powered, turbo-charged fighter planes definitely nurtured the flying bug in me. Yet even before I started studying aviation, I was interested in the way airplanes worked and hungry to learn about them. I also knew that one day, I would be behind the controls.

LIFE IN THE U.S.

I am the oldest of three children in our family, and the only one interested in pursuing a career in aviation. After graduating high school, I studied foreign affairs and political science at the Military University Nueva Granada. The plan was for me to graduate and then join the military. However, in my senior year, I decided I needed to improve my English for my future career and thought that living in the United States would be the best way to do it. I applied to an au pair program because it was significantly cheaper than an English course and I would also get the unique opportunity to be immersed in American culture by living with an American family.

In December of 2014, I started working in Chicago as an au pair. The change in language and culture was overwhelming at first. I had taken an English proficiency test to qualify for the program, but I had to learn much more, very quickly through immersion, to thrive. The family I was living with was unique. Their two kids both had autism, so it was very challenging, especially at the beginning, because I had no experience at all with their special needs. However, the kids were amazing and the part of the exchange I liked best. The hardest part, unfortunately, was working with the parents. One of the most challenging things about the au pair program is that you don't know if you and the family are a good match until you arrive. Then you must navigate personality clashes and differences for the year. Despite it all, I had a great experience and learned a lot about autism, and definitely about myself. The program took me out of my comfort zone and gave me tools to be where I am today.

My entire time in the U.S., I never forgot about flying. In fact, I would look for women pilots on social media and I found Colombian and Mexican women who were commercial pilots that I could follow as role models. I decided that someday, I would be one too.

I was also excited to see that becoming a pilot in the United States was different than it was in Colombia. Here, people get their license for recreational and hobby purposes. In Colombia, anyone in flight school is immediately transitioned into the commercial airlines or the military.

Then, before my year of being an au pair was up, I had an amazing opportunity to stay in the U.S. and help the Red Cross in community outreach. I could use my bilingual skills to counsel new immigrants through the system, conduct safe family programs, and give workshops about fire safety, prevention, etc.

in schools. I loved the work and the people I worked with and I felt I was doing something very meaningful. There was only one problem…I still wanted to fly!

Now I was 22 years old, my au pair assignment was wrapping up, and I was in a committed relationship. It was time to go home. Or was it? I knew I would have a nice life back in Colombia, but I had amazing opportunities to reach my goals and dreams in aviation if I stayed.

"Mom, dad, I'm going to stay here in the U.S."

Those were some of the hardest words I ever had to say to them because I knew I would be giving up a lot, especially time with my family. However, I've been blessed with an amazing support system and they trust my decisions because they know I don't take them lightly. I had considered the uncertainty of what the future would bring. I was leaving the known for the unknown. All my country and all the things I held dear for a new world. It was hard, but they understood that I was getting opportunities I would not have gotten back home, and they supported my decision. I knew I also still had a lot to learn about the culture here and so many other things. So, I made the move and now we keep in touch as best we can. At least once or twice a year, I either visit Colombia or my family comes and visits me here in the States.

I began looking into what it would take to get my private pilot's license in the U.S. Once again, my parents were both supportive and encouraged me to stay and achieve my goals in aviation, although my mother worries a little about how I'll ever finish it all. As she saw it, to become even a recreational pilot, I was facing three main obstacles: finances, being a Latina, and what I would do after I got my license.

MEETING THE OBSTACLES

I'm happy to say that one by one, I have checked off these obstacles as life continues to unfold.

The first obstacle was financing my flight education. I tell any Latina I know who is interested in flying that they do not have to go into the military or even a four-year college aviation program to pay for flight school. Just as people take out loans for college, I took out a loan to pay for flight school. As I did it, I was confident I would be able to become a flight instructor to help pay off the loan. I also was confident I could easily find a job as a flight instructor since they are usually in high demand. Then I could use my flight instructor hours towards my goal of becoming a commercial pilot.

The second obstacle that some people saw was being a Latina. Personally, I've never considered this an obstacle or a drawback in my career thus far, except when I first started flight school in the U.S., I realized I knew all the names of the instruments and aviation vocabulary in Spanish, but not English! In fact, I think being a woman and a Latina in this field personally helps me to try even harder to prove myself and earn the position I have as a flight instructor. I'm aware there's an attitude out there that "women don't belong in aviation," but it has never kept me from my dreams.

I do think that the lack of representation of women, (and especially Latinas), in aviation here in the U.S. presents aviation as a hard-to-reach option for young women. I'm glad to serve as a role model in this respect. When I was growing up, I saw a few women in the military, so therefore I always knew the option was open to me. When young Latinas see me, I hope they realize that they can reach their dream of flying too, just as I have. Social media is also a great way to find role models and is still a place I can go to find women like me who are doing great things in aviation!

Now that I've lived in the U.S. for some time, the language barrier is not the problem it once was, and the names of the controls in English are all second nature to me. I'm proud I can serve as a bilingual instructor, and a resource for any Latina with a dream to fly. I encourage her to come in for a discovery flight!

My mother had also worried about what I would do after I completed flight training. The answer was obvious to me. After I completed my flight training at ATP school at the DuPage Airport in 2019, I had all the ratings and requirements to become a Flight Instructor and keep working towards my dreamed Airline Pilot job.

I have now been working at ATP almost a year as a flight instructor, and I enjoy each day and what it brings. I'm honored to be able to teach other people to do what I love the most and I'm especially delighted when I'm able to teach other women. To date, I have a total of four female students, and I'm hopeful there will be more. I'm proud that what I teach them will empower them to reach their dreams in the aviation industry, and in life too.

I also enjoy the flexible hours of my job and find my work truly rewarding. Flying with students every day is exhilarating, and each lesson gives me more flight hours and brings me closer to my ultimate goal—to become a commercial pilot. In the meantime, I fly home to see my family about twice a year, but someday soon I won't be traveling in the cabin. I'll be in the cockpit, achieving my dream!

Jessika Hernandez is a flight instructor at JW Aviation. Connect with her on Instagram @jesiihernandez or jesii.hernandez@gmail. com.

COVID-19 POSTSCRIPT

I have definitely felt the effects of the pandemic in both my professional and personal life. I was furloughed from my job as a flight instructor for a month. I have returned, but the environment has changed dramatically, and I am adapting to the new "normal" for interactions with students and my fellow instructors. Social distancing is hard to do in a small cockpit; however, we all have become accustomed to flying with masks and adding an extra step to the pre-flight inspection by disinfecting the airplane.

The hardest part of all this has been the fear of the unknown in regard to the future of our careers. If you have asked me two or three months ago about the aviation industry, I would have said that it was the best time to become a pilot. Now, the future is uncertain, but it fills my heart to see my fellow pilot friends encourage each other to keep working towards our goals. We are reminded that airplanes take off against the wind and not with it, so we will overcome any hardship.

My boyfriend, who is also a pilot, has been my biggest supporter during this time. Although he lost his conditional offer to join a regional airline this summer, his uplifting spirit keeps the main goal in sight. We all believe, or hope, that this situation will be temporary, and we will all feel safe again to enjoy the wonders of our world. We know it will take some time for the industry to bounce back but in the meantime, we will be working hard so we can all keep spreading our wings and fly always higher.

LIVING THE CULTURALLY UNEXPECTED

MARIA ELENA ALVAREZ CAMPS

CURRENT POSITION
Transformation Manager at Airbus Defense & Space

FAVORITE AIRCRAFT
The Eurofighter Typhoon (of course!) Read on to find out why!

FAVORITE QUOTE
"The sun always shines, even if you do not see it
because it is hidden behind the clouds."
- Rafaela Camps, my mother

FUN FACT
I was born in Cuba, grew up in Spain, married a German in
England, and now live in Germany.

The lunar capsule of the Apollo space program that hung
above my 13-year-old head at the Johnson Space Center in

Houston set off a spark that would lead me to where I am today. I was completely amazed and had never seen anything like the spacecraft, the space suits, or the Moon rocks. It was completely inspiring to a teenage girl like me.

At the time, I was still living in Madrid with my family as political refugees from Cuba. Me and my sister, Rosa Maria, were visiting our aunt and uncle for the summer in Houston. When we returned home to Madrid, the seed was planted. All my sister talked about was wanting to become an astronaut. Since we are only 11 months apart, the school had put us in the same class when we arrived from Cuba. We did everything together. My sister's passion often became my passion as well. For me, the thought of keeping our journey together and both becoming astronauts was a perfect combination!

We knew we wanted to earn our degrees in aerospace engineering, but at the time it was only offered in America, and my parents couldn't afford it. The closest option was to study aeronautical engineering in Madrid at the only aeronautical university in Spain at the time.

STARTING THE JOURNEY

My parents knew little about the aerospace industry, as my father was an accountant and my mother was a singer in the choir of The Zarzuela of Madrid the Spanish version of an operetta. So, my father, looking for advice, invited his boss over after dinner one night to speak with us in an attempt to offer us a mentor.

"It's not a good idea for you to study aeronautical

engineering," he told us simply. He went on to explain that it was a very difficult degree and that there were very few girls in the university. Even if we did get through the studies, he said, there was only one aeronautical company in all of Spain that could hire us, making it very challenging to find a job. Then, he continued, we shouldn't worry because we could study economics or ophthalmology so that when we finished our studies we could work in his business and have an easy and secure life. My sister and I just sat there in amazement, speechless. We did not want to answer back, because at the time you were not allowed to challenge adults. So, like we usually did in moments of despair, we looked at my mother, who always told us to follow our dreams. We were relieved when she spoke up on our behalf.

"Señor I am grateful for your advice," she said politely, "but the sole reason we left Cuba with two suitcases and twenty dollars hidden in my husband's belt was so we could have freedom and our daughters could decide to be whatever they want to be. If their dream is to become aeronautical engineers, we will support them."

My dad's boss was surprised at our mother's comment, but did not press the issue. After that evening, our decision was made. We decided to pursue our dreams despite his advice.

I would like to tell you that he was entirely wrong about our future, but that wouldn't be completely true. My sister and I went on to study aeronautical engineering at la Universidad Politécnica of Madrid and indeed, the curriculum was just as difficult as my dad's boss had predicted. Coming from a small school, we did not have the background in math and science that would have made the program easier for us. And of course, we were, as he also predicted, one of only four women among 120 men. Many of our professors were from the Air Force and I still remember, as if it were yesterday, the first year my sister and I were in the office of the Dean of Technical Drawings, waiting to get our grades.

"You have both failed and you should change studies," he told us. He went on to say it would be very difficult for us to finish and even if we did, all we would ever do is "design bras" like the famous aviation engineer Howard Hughes once did.

It was the second time in a very short period that we were told we would not achieve our dreams. However, I had my parents' resilience. The Oxford definition for resilience is the capacity to recover quickly from difficulties. My interpretation of resilience is to not waste your energy hitting the wall more than once. Resilience is building a door or jumping over the wall to get where you want to be. We continued with our studies, worked hard, studied harder, and before graduating we got ourselves an internship with Construcciones Aeronatuticas Sociedad Anónima (CASA).

Upon my graduation, I continued to work at CASA as a cockpit engineer for the CN-235 military aircraft. CASA was later merged with the European Aeronautic Defense and Space Company (EADS-CASA) and later became part of Airbus Defense and Space. I felt like I had made it. I had seen plenty of aircraft and designed zero bras!

AN EXCITING PROJECT

After two years of working in Getafe, I was transferred to Warton, England, where I was an Avionics System engineer for the Eurofighter programme in the Avionics Joint Team. It was a completely different and challenging environment, working in a multinational team composed of Germans, British, Italians, and Spanish. Most of them were male, and I always remembered what Eleanor Roosevelt said: "Nobody can make you feel inferior without your consent." I pressed on, I learned, I delivered, and I started to master the intercultural environment. I also met my husband in Warton. We even got married in England and a year into our marriage, my husband was offered a better position back in Germany. Luckily, I also managed to find a job continuing in the Eurofighter programme as a flight test engineer in the Flight Control Joint Team. So, we moved back to Germany.

After one year in Germany, I had my first child, Alexander Ike, and a year later, I was pregnant with my daughter, Rosa Isabel. While being seven months pregnant with her, they offered my husband an even better position back in Warton and he took it. Those were very challenging months, having my husband abroad, while working and taking care of Alex who was 20 months old and expecting Rosa. Four months after she was born, I joined my husband in Warton, working as a test qualification engineer for the Eurofighter programme.

Guess what happened seven years later? My husband took another promotion back in Germany, and this time I transferred and received a promotion to my first manager position as Avionics

Product Manager within the Eurofighter GmbH company.

Coordinating the efforts between the four partner companies of the Eurofighter programme helped me to master an understanding of different cultures. I led a very diverse team at work and raised my son and daughter at home. All were very challenging tasks and a lot of juggling was required to manage everything. Many times, I had to use methods that were not "culturally expected" in order to achieve the targets for what I like to call my third baby, the "Eurofighter Typhoon."

The Eurofighter Typhoon is the world's most advanced swing-role combat aircraft, providing simultaneously deployable Air-to-Air and Air-to-Surface capabilities. It is powered by two EJ200 engines that give it an impressive thrust-to-weight ratio and maneuverability. It is a state-of-the-art, combat-ready weapon system that has doubled its number of original user nations since its release. One of my proudest moments was when we successfully delivered the EMAR21 (European Military Aviation Requirements) Phase 1 milestones and I had the honor of being selected as the Industry speaker at the Mutual Recognition Ceremony in January 2016. Best of all, in March 2016, I received a personal laudatory report from the General Manager of the NATO Eurofighter and Tornado Management Agency (NETMA) for my performance. It was exciting, and never boring, to be part of the development of such an incredible aircraft.

NEW DIRECTIONS

Having reached success in the Eurofighter programme, I wanted to expand my knowledge and learn about other areas of our business. For three years, I moved to the Airbus Defense and Space Headquarters in Ottobrunn, south of Germany, to work in different roles in central functions of production and engineering across the business lines.

Last year, they called me back for the Eurofighter programme to be a Transformation Manager for Airbus Spain and Germany in the newly created Joint Transformation Office. There, a group of consultants and representatives from nations and industries of the EF programme are looking to improve the current process to make the Typhoon fit for the future.

On top of my daily job, I am a great advocate of diversity. For me, it is an honor to use my corporate experience, my technical knowledge, my network and my communication and coaching skills to provide mentorship to other women interested in the aerospace industry. I am part of a group called "Balance for Business" at Airbus which embraces diversity and inclusion and organizes different activities, such as the "Direct Dialogues," where we meet physically during lunch breaks with women and men and connect virtually with other Airbus sites. We share information and bring in speakers on human and technical topics like AI, agility, finances, mindfulness, finding your "why," leadership, and much more.

Balance for Business has become so popular that we had a presence this year at the "Her Career Fair" in Munich where we explained how Airbus embraces inclusion and diversity. This event sparked interest in other women from different companies who ended up approaching me to speak and learn more about our group. I also belong to other associations outside Airbus such as the Cultural & Leadership Learning Lab, Professional Network, and Women in Big Data.

Privately I have pursued my next great passion—coaching. I am now a certified executive coach and have incorporated my coaching skills into my position with Airbus. My challenge in coaching is how to "care" about my clients in such a way that they feel safe enough to be heard and comfortable enough to be honest with themselves, so they allow me to support and challenge them to find their solutions in their journey of growth.

All in all, I'm very glad I did not let my father's boss sway me or my sister, and that we were able to follow our dreams. My sister now lives in the United States and is also enjoying a career in aviation. For me, it has been a lifetime passion that has brought me joy, a sense of accomplishment, and the opportunity to help others live a life they would never have imagined. And like I always tell my female mentees: "Remember you do not have to be perfect; you only have to be great with the resources that you have." Do not forget to enjoy every day.

Maria Elena Alvarez Camps is an executive coach and Transformation Manager at Airbus Defense & Space. She can be reached at +49176 81719300 or via Linkedin or email at campsecoaching@gmail.com.

COVID-19 POSTSCRIPT

What did I do during COVID-19? Did I exercise every day and now have a perfect bikini body? No! Did I start a new business? No! Did I learn another language or how to bake delicious cakes? No! But that is what social media was preaching to us! "Now that you have the time that you always said you didn't have, seize the opportunity to develop yourself!" In the middle of an unprecedented global crisis, the last thing I needed was social media pressure telling me that I can become better than ever.

What did I do instead? During the day, I disinfected my house while taking care of my isolated husband, who was battling COVID-19. I was mastering the art of virtual meetings from home while working on an Airbus COVID-19 project to develop a mask recycling machine. During the nights I cried a lot and prayed that my family and my parents, isolated in Madrid, would survive the nightmare.

Now, things are getting better and we are slowly going back to the NEW normal. Like I have told friends, families, and coachees during our afternoon virtual exchanges, this experience has taught me to be to be compassionate to myself and others, and to be grateful for my present and all the little things that I may never have noticed before.

MARIA LASKOWSKI

CURRENT POSITION
Multinational Account Manager, Aeroméxico

FAVORITE AIRCRAFT
Boeing 787 Dreamliner
More space, more amenities…it's beautiful!

FAVORITE QUOTE
"Traeume nicht dein Leben, sondern lebe deine Traeume"
(Don't dream your life; live your dreams!)

FUN FACT
I met my husband in Vegas.

It was July 31, 2018, and I was working as a Market Manager for Aeroméxico. I had traveled to Mexico City for a meeting and was stepping into an elevator when one of my coworkers turned to me and said the words everyone who works at an airline never wants to hear.

"There's been an accident," she said.

One of our planes, Flight 2421, had been taking off in Durango, Mexico bound for Mexico City when a sudden wind shear caused by a microburst hit the plane just as it became airborne off the runway. The plane quickly lost speed and altitude. The left wing struck the runway, and the engines detached, taking the plane down and catching fire. All 103 people on board survived, but 39 passengers and crew members were injured.

I was in shock. I felt like I couldn't breathe. Working in the airline industry, you know things like this are possible, but you never, ever expect them. My heart went out to those poor people. This was a nightmare, within an industry that makes people's dreams come true!

LESSONS FROM THE INDUSTRY

I've always considered air travel and the airline industry to be a magical, safe place that takes people to the places they most want to go. Nobody likes to get to the airport two hours before a flight, so they have enough time to park their car, get through security, check bags, etc., but the reasons why they do it make it all worthwhile. Our customers are excited to be traveling to visit friends for the first time in a long time. They're expectant businessmen anticipating the close of a long-awaited deal, loving couples on their way to a joyous honeymoon, nervous parents bringing home their adopted babies, happy families off to a warm, sunny beach vacation, and rowdy athletes traveling to the championship game. Those of us who work for the airlines unknowingly play a part in these everyday miracles, thanks to airline travel.

Even when the reason for travel is sad—a trip to a funeral, to see a sick friend, or to see a specialist for a serious illness—the ability to attend these life-changing, memorable, one-in-a-lifetime events is possible because of the availability of air travel.

It's almost destiny that I work in a multicultural environment like the airlines because I was born and raised in a unique multicultural environment in Mexico City. My mother's people were from Germany, so I grew up speaking German as well as Spanish. I even attended German school. I grew up with the traditional songs and lullabies of someone born in Germany, and I thought it was a wonderfully unique thing about our family.

When I graduated college with my degree in marketing, I aspired to work at a German company so I could use my language skills. My first job, however, was as a marketing coordinator in the automotive industry. When a friend called me and told me about an opening at Aeroméxico for an international marketing group, I jumped at the chance.

Someone told me, once you have a job in the airline industry, you won't leave. For me, that was somewhat correct. I remember being at a photo shoot of our jets. I remember standing there, watching them water the floors so that the gleaming airplane would reflect dramatically in the picture. I love this industry, I thought. It didn't matter that we had to be at the hangar at four o'clock in the morning so we could get the plane out and ready for the photographer to shoot it at sunrise. It was all splendid and glamorous. I traveled a lot and had a chance to use my German in Europe, and also met people and clients from Germany, too.

I started at Aeroméxico at an interesting time. The H1N1 virus was gripping the world, and unfortunately, in Mexico, we were at the epicenter. It was 2009, and air travel had come to a screeching halt. I was working in the marketing department and we were told we had a "zero budget" for marketing. For the airline to survive, we would also need to take a 15 percent pay cut and continue to do our job of communicating to the public that our airline was still running and safe to fly. One of the most common misconceptions we had to combat was the belief that our aircrafts' air was unhealthy and perpetuating the virus. The truth was that our aircraft completely recycled the cabin air many times an hour. So how could we get our messages out without a budget?

We reached out to the Mexican tourism board and hotels who were also suffering from the bad publicity and the decrease in air travel because of the virus. We worked with an ad agency, and although we could not pay them, we gave them free airline tickets. At the time, our big competitor was Air Mexicana and they were not quite as resourceful as we were. They soon declared bankruptcy and closed their doors, another victim of the H1N1 virus.

The important lesson I learned from that experience is that when times are difficult, you must see the potential in everything and everybody around you. There's always a way.

FLYING HOME

I tried working in a few other industries between 2010 and 2013, but I ended up back in aviation. Deep down, I think it's where I belonged. Then in 2012, I met my American husband on a vacation in Las Vegas and he was the catalyst for my ultimate move to the U.S. He always jokes that what happens in Vegas doesn't stay in Vegas. It follows you home and becomes your wife and the mother of your children. We've been married five years now.

So, after hearing about Flight 2421 in that elevator that fateful day in July, I made my way back to the hotel and turned on the news. The story was breaking across the channels, and our boss had told us not to speak to anyone about the accident. Soon we found out that the crash was a caused by a combination of factors including weather conditions, crew and air traffic controller error, and inadequate equipment.

A few hours later, I received a call from the airline with a special assignment. There was a family aboard Flight 2421 that consisted of a mother, father, a little boy about three years old, and two daughters, aged eight and ten. They were from Chicago but had been on their way home when the accident occurred. The younger daughter's body had been burned eighty percent and the father and other sister had sustained bad injuries as well. They had been airlifted to a hospital in Chicago, near the family's home, for the proper medical treatment and the mother and little boy needed to return to the city that day. Since I spoke Spanish and was from the U.S., the airline asked me to accompany them to Chicago as a representative of the airline, but also for moral support.

When I spotted them at the airport, I was a little nervous. I didn't know whether the mother was going to take her anger out on me somehow, since I was a representative of the airline. After all, she had every right to be angry at us, the planes, and her injured loved ones. Instead, I met a very gracious, strong woman, standing taller and stronger than you would expect from the victim of a tragedy, and holding the hand of a quiet, but happy little boy. I introduced myself and soon it was time to board the plane.

Once aboard, I concentrated on keeping the little boy occupied so the mother could have time to process everything. The boy and I became fast friends, but I could tell he was scared and tried to distract him as much as possible. Just before take-off he turned to me.

"This plane will not fall down, right?" he asked. My heart went out to him at that moment. I knew he would be living with his experience for some time.

Nevertheless, I distracted him by talking and singing Christian songs which seemed to amuse the boy and keep the mother's courage up. The mother told me all about her husband and her children. After a while, she even talked to me about the accident, and how in the chaos neither she nor her husband were able to get to her daughter in time. It weighed heavily on her heart and all I could do to comfort her was to listen and pray with her for the little girl she would soon be with again.

When we landed, she asked me to accompany her to the hospital to see the rest of her family. The request surprised me since I expected they would want their privacy, but at the same time I was honored that she would even think to include me. By now, I felt as if I knew the family and I did want to meet them. I also wanted assurance that they would be alright.

At the hospital, the scene, while sad, was also one of the most beautiful things I ever witnessed. Despite the circumstances, the family was in pure joy at seeing one another again. As I watched the tenderness and devotion, even between the small siblings, I knew that this tragedy had bound them together more closely than ever before. The mother introduced me, and the family received me as a gift, not an enemy. The father even thanked me for flying with his family. I felt good knowing that they were receiving great care in the hospital and I also knew they would be ok emotionally; they had each other!

FAMILIAL LOVE

I wrote this story while on maternity leave, having welcomed my first child, my little son Noah, into the world. I think of that strong family from the accident and find them an inspiration for what I want my family to be, too. I'm still adjusting to being a mom, and I'm currently handling more diapers than Fortune 500 accounts as I transition back to work. I'm grateful, though, that my work with the airline allowed me to bring my mom and sister here for Noah's birth. It also allowed us to travel back home to Mexico, where all my family resides, so he was able to experience their love as well.

Now that I've resumed my career as a Multinational Account Manager for Aeromexico, I'm learning to fit the fast pace of my work into my new role as a mother. The return to work came with a change in my role and new challenges, but It doesn't matter whether I stay in the same position or grow, as long as I can be the working mom I want to be.

In my life, I've been blessed to be surrounded by miracles—everyday small ones at the airline, and now, a truly life transforming one called motherhood. I'm grateful for it all and look forward to more miracles, great and small. I'm ready to receive them all.

Maria Laskowski is a Multinational Account Manager at Aeroméxico. She can be reached at linkedin.com/in/maria-laskowski.

COVID POSTSCRIPT

COVID-19 hit just after I returned to work on March 2 from being on maternity leave for three months. I was just starting a new position as Multinational Account Manager with Aeromexico when they told me I was furloughed for one month, beginning April 13. So yes, after six weeks of being back at work, I was off once again. Now the furlough time has been extended until July 15 and we don't know yet if it will be extended even more.

The good news is that I have had time to see Noah grow and be with him, so the timing worked well as a new mom. My baby is now six months old and I have been with him, almost non-stop, his entire life, except for the six weeks I was back at work.

I wish my family and friends could visit and enjoy him too, but despite not being able to leave the house, I love having time to be a full-time mom at this early stage of his life.

LIZBETH ALVARADO

CURRENT POSITION

Air Traffic Controller, O'Hare International Airport

FAVORITE AIRCRAFT

B1 Lancer

It's a heavy aircraft that maneuvers like a fighter plane!

FAVORITE QUOTE

"Life doesn't always turn out like we expect it, and that's OK!"

FUN FACT

I work in a tower even though I'm afraid of heights.

You never forget the conversations that change your life and put you on a track towards success. I remember being a young mom, out of high school, and figuring out my next move in life. I was working full-time, trying to continue my education, and struggling to support my adorable son, Einar (pronounced Ay-Nar). His smile and joy were compelling me to do more, be more, and of course, support him well. His name was of Viking origin and meant "leader of warriors". I wanted to give him a life that allowed him to develop the strength and fearlessness that his name gave him.

One day my two cousins told me they were planning on joining the Air Force. One wanted to be a pilot and the other one wanted to become a doctor. The more they talked about it, the more I started to consider military service too. Joining the military would give me a place in life, a well-paying, steady job and best of all, the chance to attend college after service was up.

MILITARY TRAILBLAZER

I had no role model for military service. None of my immediate family had ever served. However, my upbringing definitely influenced me in making the decision. I was taught that hard work, along with education, was the key to success. I was also taught responsibility, professionalism, and to have a strong work ethic, which I still carry with me to this day. So, I started talking to a recruiter about my options and before I knew it, I had enlisted in the U.S. Air Force. My family was surprised, but very proud that I had made the decision to serve my country. In the end, both of my cousins ended up not enlisting and took different paths to fulfill their dreams. I did, and it was a move that led me to a career in aviation that suits me perfectly!

I was twenty when I joined the U.S. Air Force, with the idea that service would be a means to an end. My plan was to get some military experience, then attend college after discharge where

I would find my lifetime career. But the Air Force gave me an aptitude test to see how I could best serve them. When I got the results, I didn't know what to expect, since I was open to almost anything. I was so surprised and intrigued when one of the job recommendations turned out to be "air traffic controller" (ATC). I decided to give it a try.

I completed basic training in San Antonio, Texas and then a vocational school in Biloxi, Mississippi to learn the basics of air traffic control. I was then assigned to Dyess Air Force Base in Abilene, Texas where I continued my ATC training. I worked and served in the Air Force for four years.

The aptitude test was right! I really enjoyed the work of air traffic controlling. I see it as a game of chess. Pieces in motion, trying to get to a specific spot with different variables creating a different puzzle to solve with each new move. I loved the variety of military aircraft and their requirements as they came through the base. No two days were the same and it was a job that kept you on your toes.

I also have to say that the job fit my personality very well. While you'll find many different types of personalities among air traffic controllers (ATCs), they do share many qualities and personality characteristics. For example, I think ninety-nine percent of ATCs have a type A personality. They are also great multi-taskers and very detail-oriented individuals. In your busiest moments as an ATC, you don't always have to multi-task, but you do have to think and solve problems quickly. You also have to be adaptable. You have to solve any issues and move on. Through my work I developed confidence and the skill to make fast decisions and pivot when the situation calls for it.

I believe it takes a village to raise a child, and the military was part of the village that helped me raise Einar. They were surprisingly family friendly. I always had daycare available, right on the base, and was even able to leave work hours early to attend school functions as long as it did not compromise the mission.

After my service was up, I returned home to Chicago. I had really missed it and I wanted Einar to grow up near family. I also figured I would take advantage of my veteran's benefits and attend school. I thought about my options and decided to try something different—nursing.

FINDING MY CAREER

I was in college for about a year when I started to miss the excitement of aviation and using those skills I had worked so hard to build in the Air Force. I thought long and hard about my decision. I had decided on nursing to build a career for myself but my longing for aviation made me realize I already had a career—air traffic control. In the military I had not just received job experience; I had found my lifelong career.

People had told me that if you were looking for a job as an air traffic controller, chances are that you will not find one near home. I was still determined to try because at this point in life, I knew I didn't want to move and uproot Einar again. In the summer of 2007, I saw that the FAA was hiring. I applied and was hired! Even better, I was given the "Holy Grail" of assignments. I was placed in the air traffic control tower at Midway Airport in Chicago.

Although smaller than O'Hare, Midway airport is still ranked among the top thirty busiest airports in the country. The first few days were a little nerve-wracking, but I persevered. Eventually, the job got easier, even though I was still challenged on a day-to-day basis. Commercial operations were much more involved than the military ones I was used to back at Dyess.

There, we flew about 200 daily operations out of the military base. Midway had more than four times that amount, at about 800 operations a day. At Midway, the traffic was very different from the military too. At Dyess, we would do our training and then work with one or two aircraft at a time, usually a cargo or bomber aircraft. In the commercial world, things are much more fast-paced.

When people board a commercial airliner, very few realize how many air traffic controllers (ATCs) are involved in their flight. There is one ATC assigned to help get the pilot from the gate to the runway, another for departure, and then several more throughout the flight as the pilot enters different airspaces, states, altitudes, and distances from and to the destination. It's a constant relay of information between the pilot and the ATCs. People also think of ATCs as the people in the towers, but there are whole ATC facilities elsewhere that passengers never see. The ATCs in the radar environment use only radar to direct the traffic and are just as essential as the ATCs who work in the towers.

I worked at Midway for six years when a job opened up at O'Hare Tower. Einar was now a teenager so I thought this would be a good time to apply. I was selected and transferred to O'Hare two years later. O'Hare is one of the world's busiest airports that does an average of 2,800 operations a day. ATCs are known as having high-stress jobs, and airports like O'Hare are one of the reasons why! The sheer volume of aircraft that moves through the field is challenging in and of itself. Sometimes I feel like we cannot talk fast enough to move all the planes! Yet working as a team we move them all, day after day, bringing passengers safely home or off to exciting visits and vacations. Today, I'm in the tower at O'Hare, enjoying the non-stop action and keeping air travel safe.

THE JOY OF ATC

I've been living with the pace and the internal stress of the job for a while now, and I guess I'm accustomed to it. It's the kind of stress that doesn't leave me anxious at the end of the day but might settle in my neck or shoulders and in need of a massage! Still, it's a career I love. In the military, I was serving the country. Now in civilian life, I'm serving an industry that has made us possible to stay connected and make important things happen around the world.

It's also a career that enabled me to support my son, who today is 19 and has grown into a young man who lives up to his name. Looking back, I can say that he was my main inspiration to always be moving forward in life towards a better goal. Certainly, I wouldn't have been as focused on getting a career and becoming an ATC at one of the world's busiest airports if it hadn't been for my passion for aviation and for supporting my family.

I'm glad I found ATC, or should I say, it found me.

Lizbeth Alvarado is an air traffic controller at O'Hare International Airport. She can be reached on Facebook and LinkedIn as Lizbeth Alvarado.

COVID-19 POSTSCRIPT

These days it is surreal to report to work at one of the country's busiest airports and find it so empty. The coronavirus and resulting stay at home order is so evident by our drop in volume and passengers. As an essential worker, I still report to work my shift, but our operations are running at about twenty-five to thirty percent. We are now divided into three teams, so that if one team has a member who is ill, the entire team can isolate and be relieved by a backup team.

The cargo aircraft seem to have a new meaning to me, knowing they are transporting critical supplies or even packages for people eagerly anticipating them at home. I also watch the commercial flights take off and think that these trips must be seriously important to be traveling during this difficult time. As ATCs, we can never forget how important each flight is to the passenger. Everyone on the plane is a passenger or flight crew member that is loved, missed, or anticipated by another loved one. It's our job to get them where they need to go as safely as possible, even in the midst of a pandemic.

SUSANA LISSETTE IBARRA CÁCERES

CURRENT POSITION
First Officer, Kuwait Airways

FAVORITE AIRCRAFT
Airbus350. Beautiful, spacious, sophisticated and my dream airplane to fly!

FAVORITE QUOTE
"The strongest actions for a woman is to love herself, be herself, and shine amongst those who never believed she could."
—Unknown

FUN FACT
Life takes you to unexpected, amazing places. If someone told me years ago that I'd one day be living in Kuwait, flying for Kuwait Airways, I would never have believed them. And yet, here I am doing it.

I have many people to thank for this accomplishment, but most of all, my mother, Lis Cáceres. She's an incredible woman; a civil war survivor who successfully immigrated to the United States and raised four girls, virtually on her own. She's also survived breast cancer and encouraged and supported me every step of the way in what has been a very unconventional journey.

DESTINATION COCKPIT

When I was a little girl growing up in El Salvador, my father had a great interest in aviation and becoming a pilot. He used to take me to air shows and would share his dream of learning to fly, although this never came to be. Instead, he served in the military but never became a pilot.

For me, I had other dreams other than becoming a pilot when I was young. After graduating high school, I went on to the university to study international relations. I thought about becoming an ambassador or serving in some role where I could empower women. I didn't know exactly what I would do but I wanted to do something of significance, that helped advance the rights of women.

I was 19 years old and on a break from the university when I answered an advertisement to become a flight attendant for Avianca El Salvador (TACA). I thought it sounded fun and could be a temporary job I would do for the three months of the break. Instead, I ended up truly enjoying the work and staying on. For the first six months, I was happy in the role, but after a while, I started spending less time in the back of the airplane and closer up front near the cockpit. I finally faced the realization that it is where I wanted to be. I didn't want to be serving and sitting back with the passengers; I wanted to be flying the plane and sitting in the cockpit. Yes, I was starting to think about becoming a pilot.

At that time, there were absolutely no women pilots in El Salvador. None. I started asking around for advice on how I could become a pilot and I was actively discouraged by everyone—pilots who worked at the airlines, fellow flight attendants, friends, and family. There were no role models for women pilots and apparently nobody even thought it was possible. Nobody, except my family. My mom told me I should look for a pilot school, and that is exactly what I did.

My first, one-hour flight with an instructor was all it took to know that my instincts were right—I wanted to be a pilot and I would do anything I needed to do to make it happen. But getting a license was expensive. My mother worried about how we could afford it and she wanted me to wait a bit. Instead, I went to a bank and was able to secure a loan from a bank to cover the cost of training to receive my private pilot's license. It relieved her of the pressure to pay for me and allowed me to start working towards my dream goal.

FORGING AHEAD

My commitment to my goal and my persistence surprised everyone, even me. My ground training class was full of men who were surprised and shocked at my presence in the class. Some of them were expecting me to fail. They even joked about it, but I wouldn't let them, or anything else, keep me from my goal. The area surrounding Ilopango International Airport in El Salvador was very dangerous, especially at five o'clock in the morning when I usually needed to be there, but I was committed to my goal of becoming a commercial airline pilot.

In 2008, my mother moved to Los Angeles, California in the U.S. with my youngest sister, Rocío, after she and my father separated. As I am the oldest in the family, my sisters Paola and Melissa stayed behind in El Salvador with me. My mother and I were both supportive of each other's life plans, and she pledged her support to keep helping me work towards my goal of becoming a commercial pilot. My father was away from us at that time, but he too was happy with what I was trying to accomplish. In the U.S., my mother continued to work tirelessly as a domestic worker and sent me checks to help me get my instrument license, and eventually, my commercial license.

Next, I faced the daunting goal of getting 1,200 hours to become a commercial pilot. So, I became a flight instructor and started my slow journey towards accumulating the hours I needed. I was still going to school too, and because I was a new instructor, there were weeks I would only be in the air one or two hours a week. For a while, I endured my slow progress, telling myself it wasn't a competition or race and I would finish when I finished. But eventually, I couldn't take it anymore. I needed to find another way to progress more quickly.

I found a job with La Costeña, a small, Nicaraguan airline, flying a Cessna Caravan 208. There, I flew mainly to Costa Rica and the islands and remote cities of Nicaragua. I flew nearly every day and in two years, I had racked up 1,500 hours of flight time and was ready to bring my experience back to El Salvador. However, I found trailblazing into the male world of aviation to be harder than I ever imagined.

By 2014, I had earned my commercial pilot's license and accumulated more than enough hours to qualify me for a position in TACA airlines, yet somehow, I could not get hired there. Some pilots in charge of recruitment told me to come back when I had more hours, even though they were hiring men with fewer hours than I had. It was completely demoralizing.

For a while I wondered if everyone was right and if my dream was unreachable after all? I considered quitting and going to Los Angeles to be with the rest of my family, but I could not overlook the unfairness of it all. There were women pilots in Guatemala, Costa Rica, Honduras, and Colombia. Why not El Salvador? I knew I was as competent as any man. I still had big dreams and could picture myself as captain of a commercial airliner, flying people around the world. Yet, my rejection from the airlines within my home country made me feel rather small and unaccomplished. I think I spent a month in my room, depressed, not knowing what to do next, just trying to find a way to keep going. Then God heard my prayers.

ANOTHER WORLD, ANOTHER GOAL

In 2014, a new airline, Vuelos Economicos de Centro America, VECA, opened up. They had hired some of the pilots

I had worked with at TACA and recommended me to VECA. Before I knew it, I was hired as the first officer of the Airbus 319. We trained in Miami, Florida with the best instructors I could ask for, at the Airbus training center. It was a dream come true for me.

Unfortunately, VECA folded due to financial problems in 2017. It was a sad time for me and my colleagues. But by then, the world was open to me. I was in a good position to be hired at AVIANCA the only airline in my country, but luckily for me, it did not happen. Instead, I expanded my horizons and investigated my global options. I applied to airlines like EVA AIR in Asia and I was rejected immediately, just for being a woman. I had friends who were employed with airlines in the Middle East like Kuwait Airways, Qatar Airways, or Emirates and spoke very highly of them. They encouraged me to apply there and I received an interview with Kuwait Airways. When I flew to Istanbul for the interview, I was hired on the spot! I didn't really know it at the time, but I was to become the second female pilot in the history of the airline. But first, I had to move to Kuwait.

Making the move to the Middle East was a major adjustment and scary too. Everything about life changed. I arrived in Kuwait in the summer of 2017 when the temperature was unbearably hot, topping one hundred and twenty-degrees every day. It was also Ramadan, a Muslim religious observance and period of fasting from sunrise to sunset, with no eating or drinking in public.

The first two weeks I had fevers and headaches. I was

homesick, so far away from friends and family. I also experienced a couple of historically strong sandstorms, where the sand completely covers cars and it became difficult to breathe and sleep, even inside, because of all the sand.

I had to adapt to the dress code, keeping myself covered in public (or risk harassment), and customs like not shaking hands or making eye contact. I also am still learning Arabic and getting better at it every day.

At work the training on my new aircraft was tough and I had to learn to work with Arab men, some of whom at first refused to fly with a woman and did not take me seriously. I was somewhat used to this from my home country; as a woman pilot, I was always being tested and evaluated for my competency. I needed to prove my worth as I have with every other plane I've commanded. Today I fly the Airbus 320 to destinations like Rome, Munich, Mumbai, Delhi, Frankfurt, Vienna, Geneva, Beirut, Istanbul, Dubai, Qatar, Pakistan, Egypt, and Saudi Arabia. Now, my coworkers know what I can do and respect me for it. Even though my on-the-job performance is not about them, I believe if you first impress yourself, you'll naturally impress others.

Now my next goal is one I want to reach for women everywhere, and that's to become the first "expat" female captain at Kuwait Airways. An expat is someone not native to the country and since arriving, I've learned that the airline has never upgraded an expat from first officer to captain. Now, that is my goal. I envision myself upgrading to a Boeing 777 or Airbus 330 or 350, and if I get the chance, I'll be ready for it.

Even though it hasn't been easy, I'm proud to be a woman in the industry, blazing a trail in this part of the world. However, I don't know how long I'll be at the airlines. I don't like to think that I will be first officer forever, and I know I'm in the top ten in seniority right now. I'd like to be here long enough to qualify and fight for a position as a female captain. We'll see what happens.

In the meantime, I'm looking forward to my upcoming marriage to a wonderful Australian man I met here in Kuwait, and I'm grateful for everything that has come my way. I'm especially grateful to my family, mother and sisters, who have supported me economically and emotionally to make my dreams come true. Now, the airlines and pilots in El Salvador know me and I'm proud to be a role model for women internationally so they know that there is room for them in the aviation world too. I've enjoyed conquering different challenges in my own way. Are there even more worlds to conquer in my future? I hope so!

Susana Lissette Ibarra Cáceres is a First Officer of the Airbus 320 for Kuwait Airways. She can be reached at susanalibarrac@ gmail.com or at Instagram @susanaibarracaceres.

THREE'S A CHARM

JACQUELINE PRENCES VALLE

CURRENT POSITION

Internationally Certified Pilot & Owner of Nevería
Michoacána, LLC

FAVORITE AIRCRAFT

Cessna 210. I have so many good memories of that plane!

FAVORITE QUOTE

"We must accept finite disappointment, but never lose infinite hope."-
- Martin Luther King Jr.

FUN FACT

I personally make all the popsicles we sell at my business.

One of my fondest childhood memories was flying with my
father. Growing up in Buenos Aires, Argentina, my dad worked
as an exporter in the plastics industry, but he had his pilot's

license too. On the weekends, he would take little trips to places that were a few hours away from our home, like the lovely town of Mar del Plata. He would usually take at least one of his four children with him, and since I was the oldest, it was often me.

I was only four years old when he got his license, but I remember the joy it brought him. The first time he took me up in his aircraft, I was completely smitten with flight. Eventually, my father bought his own Cessna 210 and he would fly it nearly every weekend. When I was six years old and we were taking one of our weekend jaunts, I remember turning to him and saying, "Papi, I'm going to be a pilot too!" He kindly smiled at me in that way parents do when their children say something cute, but ridiculous. "Ok," he replied.

STILL THE DREAM

Even when I was young, I understood the downside and risks of becoming a pilot. I remember one day when we set out for Saladillo Provincia de Buenos Aires and it looked like a great day to fly. As we journeyed though, the sky began to change. Then the rain began and before we knew it, we were in the middle of an unexpected, full-throttle thunderstorm. We rocked mercilessly in the turbulence and I saw my father grappling at the controls. I tried to keep quiet so he could concentrate but then he turned to me and said, "We're going to have to make an emergency landing." Even at my young age I knew that couldn't be a good thing, and what's more, I also knew it would be harder in a thunderstorm than any other time.

I held on tight as I watched my dad navigate the storm. He did everything right. He didn't change power settings; he selected the setting for reduced airspeed and maintained a constant altitude as he let the aircraft "ride the waves." I wasn't as worried about crashing as I was about the lightning strikes. Every flash of light through the windscreen was terrifying to me. Then, I could feel us descending. He had found a field and we were going to try to land. I braced myself and held on tight as dad guided the aircraft as gently as he could to a ragged, bumpy stop. Amazingly, we were both ok, but it was a memory I would never forget.

It didn't dim my hopes to become a pilot, though. Especially after that experience, my dad thought I was just kidding about my goal, but as I grew, so did my passion for flight.

In my senior year, I remember going to an orientation about different careers. That day just sealed my dream to become a commercial airline pilot. I went home and talked to my dad seriously about letting me learn to fly so I could become an airline pilot. Dad looked a little hesitant and seemed to be thinking hard about how best to answer me. "Jackie," he began, "I know you love flying, but it's not a job. It's just a hobby. You are going to get a family and what would be best for you is to keep it as a hobby."

I was so conflicted at his words. I loved my dad so much but what he said had upset me. He was basically saying I couldn't be a commercial airline pilot because there were just too few opportunities for women. It just didn't seem fair. However, with his blessing, I still pursued flight training. At the time, it was the most I could do to work towards my goal.

At that time in Argentina, there were two parts to getting my license, just as there is in the U.S. today. There was the classroom and test portion and then the practical flight training and testing. I worked hard with a passion that even surprised my family. I received my pilot's license on December 19, 1991. I was 18 years old. Then I pursued a license to fly gliders, which are planes without an engine. It was the last license I pursued in Argentina, but boy, did I put my license to good use. I would fly to our family farm on the weekend, and one of my fondest flying memories is a trip I took with six of my girlfriends when I was 19.

There I was, behind the controls, flying with my friends to Isla Martin Garcia. Among our group of friends, I was always regarded as the wild and weird one. Now I was proving it! We were all so excited. Just the six of us, no parents. We made the most of every moment of that weekend, eating out, laying on the beach, and going dancing at night. All made possible from my pilot's license!

NEW HORIZONS

In school, I was studying educational science, but my dreams never wavered from becoming an airline pilot. My sister, on the other hand, wanted to go to college at the University of Berkeley in California. When she got accepted, my father thought an early retirement was in order and he moved the family to California in 2000. I was married by then and about the same time, my then-husband received a job offer from Lucent

Technologies in Naperville, Illinois, outside of Chicago. Off we went to the U.S. along with our family.

To my surprise, I found out that in the U.S. I was not certified to fly! Since I held a current, international license, I thought I was all set, but I found out that I needed to be recertified in the U.S. I needed to fill out a verification of license form and visit a local flight safety district to schedule an interview with a designated pilot examiner so they could verify my identity and documents. Then I needed to demonstrate my English language proficiency and make a small payment to receive my temporary airman's certificate.

I was a little disappointed with the delay in getting back to flying, but I concentrated on other areas of my life---including motherhood! In 2007 I gave birth to Caleb, and then in 2011 had my second son, Levi. As they grew, I was sad that I could not share my flight with them, but I knew my day would come.

After his project ended in Naperville, my husband accepted a position in Mexico City, and we moved there. The best part about living in Mexico was that getting my pilot's license in Mexico was relatively easy compared to the U.S.! I met with an instructor, practiced fewer than 50 landings with about 15 hours of flying time, and then I was certified as a private pilot in Mexico.

It was wonderful to have my wings again, this time in Mexico. I could even bring my boys on some flights as well. We were in Mexico City for four years. Unfortunately, during that time things in my marriage changed, and I decided to return to the U.S. to be closer to family. I settled into the Chicago area as a single mother, and found a job teaching at the College of DuPage, a large nearby community college.

Then one day my brother had an interesting offer for me.

"Hey, want to buy an ice cream shop and run it with me?" he asked.

I almost laughed out loud because I knew absolutely nothing about the ice cream business, but I did see it as a brand-new challenge. We ended up buying and opening Nevería Michoacána, LLC a Mexican-style ice cream shop in Bolingbrook, Illinois. We are now in our second year of operating the business, and things are going well. If you've never tried Michoacána, it's very much like gelato, or Italian ice cream. At our store, we use all fresh fruit to make the great flavors of mango, orange, banana, etc. It's true that everything tastes better when it's fresher, and that's what we offer at our shop!

Today, I'm an ice cream purveyor, not an airline pilot, but yes, I still think about flying as I'm making paletas (popsicles). My dream remains to get my pilot's license in the U.S. and be able to claim a pilot's license in three countries! I've been delayed, but I'm planning to pursue my recertification in the next few months. The sky is always there waiting for me, and I'll be back soon. Wish me luck!

Jacqueline Prences Valle is owner of Nevería Michoacána in Bolingbrook, Illinois. Contact her at jprencesvalle@gmail.com.

COVID-19 POSTSCRIPT

The pandemic has affected everyone on multiple levels, and it has particularly impacted me on a personal and economic level. Similar to the new reality we faced after September eleventh, I'm certain this pandemic will bring about a new reality for all of us.

I was saddened to lose one of my greatest aviation mentors, Carlos Alberto Lalin, who passed away on April 13. He was an incredible pilot who taught my father to fly, and like so many people who died during this quarantine, he did not receive the funeral he deserved.

Right now, I am once again delaying the pursuit of my private pilot's license in the United States. I am not discouraged about it, though. I know there are better times ahead.

CHANGING THE CONVERSATION

ANA URIBE-RUIZ

CURRENT POSITION
Co-President, Bay Area Chapter, Women in Aviation
International

FAVORITE AIRCRAFT
Piper Archer II
I like the low wing planes!

FAVORITE QUOTE
"The sky is never the limit; it's the beginning of a journey!"
It's my personal motto!

FUN FACT
Back in Ecuador, I was a ballerina for eighteen years and even
danced professionally.

I live in the Bay Area near San Francisco, California, in a
land of beautiful weather where a pilot like me can fly almost

every day. The view from above displays the gorgeous diversity of the state's landscape, from the sparkling ocean to the crystal mountain tops and the parched deserts. As much as I love flying myself, I'm just as excited to motivate the next generation. I enjoy helping them explore aviation so they too, can experience the joy that I do at the controls of a plane.

PARENT PILOTS

Compared to some pilots, I'm relatively new to the sport, but I've always been surrounded by aviation. I was raised on it, back in my days growing up in Quito, Ecuador. My father and some investors had formed an airline in the late 1950's that quickly became the country's flagship aviation provider. It was called Ecuatoriana de Aviacion.

My father was an air traffic expert. He was the type of air traffic expert who understood everything about what it took to get a plane from point A to point B, including how many hours it would take and how much fuel he would need. He traveled frequently, so I had plenty of time in the cockpit with him. My childhood days were spent taking quick trips, like little three-day vacations, to destinations like Mexico. I remember my two brothers and I packing an extra change of clothes on these trips, just in case we were able to stay a little longer and enjoy the new vistas. The flexibility of airline travel was a wonderful perk for us.

After high school, I attended law school in Ecuador, then moved to the U.S. to study finance. I settled in Florida and became a banker. Eventually, I transitioned to private investment banking which involved working internationally. I had plenty of travel throughout Guatemala, Mexico, El Salvador, and other parts of South America. It was not long before I was giving my all to my career. I was working almost every day of the week, and it was hard to meet people. Then one day I went over to a friend's house and she was talking to one of her friends on the phone. They seemed to be having a good time, and I told her the person on the other end sounded like a lot of fun.

"Here, you talk to him a while," my friend said, handing me the phone. So, I did.

His name was Daniel and he was from Costa Rica and living in New Jersey. I really enjoyed talking to him. He called the next day and we found out we had a lot in common. Believe it or not, Daniel loved aviation, too, and he was already a private pilot. We talked for two hours! Then, we started talking to each other almost daily. Six months later, I went to visit him in New Jersey. Five days later, we started planning our lives together. We've now been married for twenty years!

In 2000, we were living in New Jersey when we welcomed our son, Jose-Maria, into our family. Jose-Maria has autism, and I was grateful that the school system had a good program for him. Eventually though, his need for therapy increased. I left my career to devote myself to his care and to be able to be present in his accomplishments.

In 2009, my husband was transferred to California and we moved there. It was somewhat of an adjustment. Everything was a lot more expensive and I was used to a closer, tighter, community. People seemed more independent on the west coast. However, the school was good for my son. Eventually, I became a paraeducator for special needs children in the school district. I enjoyed being able to give parents the benefit of my experience raising Jose-Maria, and to help children with challenges like his.

For Daniel, one of the perks of living in California was the wonderful flying weather. He wanted to become a commercial IFR-rated pilot, one who can fly in the clouds with instruments only, and he needed to get the required hours. He started to fly on the weekends, and we would often all go together as a family. After a while, I figured since I was now flying with him so often, it made sense for me to get my license too. We also figured it made sense to buy our own plane rather than keep renting one for my training and Daniel's flying hours, so together we purchased a Piper Archer II. The first time I went flying with an instructor I realized what Daniel had been so excited about all these years! It was a life-changing moment.

It was 2011 and I was in my forties when I got my private pilot's license. As I started to learn more about women in aviation, I was shocked to hear how rare our representation was within the profession. For example, only six percent of commercial airline pilots are women. I guess since I had grown up with aviation, I had not thought about the many little girls out there who may have aspired to a career in aviation, but had no role models, or encouragement to pursue aviation as a career. I decided to do something about it.

INSPIRING THE YOUNG

After a little research, I contacted Women of Aviation International Week (IWOAW) and organized a Women of Aviation Week celebration at San Carlos airport in the Bay Area. For me, it was a way of helping introduce young women to the opportunities awaiting them in the world of aviation.

I approached the IWOAW as a way to introduce girls, especially those in minority groups, to a branch of STEM. The careers based in the world of aviation touch many branches of science including math, science, meteorology, physics, and aeronautics. Plus, a career in aviation extends beyond pilots. You could be an engineer, a mechanic, air traffic controller, dispatcher, work with the FAA, or in several other jobs that keep our country in the air and flying safely. I wanted the girls of this generation to know all that awaited them if they were interested.

Typically, IWOAW is usually held the first week of the month in March to commemorate the month that the first pilot's license was issued to a woman, Raymonde de Laroche of France in 1910. Together with some fellow pilots from a local flying club, I put together an event at San Carlos airport in the Bay Area for March 8-10, 2013. A healthy group of about fifty middle-school and high-school aged girls from around the area came to learn about aviation and of course, to get an experience flying with a private pilot.

I've found that if you get a group of Latina and African American girls from low- income families in a room and ask them what they want to be when they graduate, about seventy percent of them will say they want to join the police force or be a social worker. I know that their answers reflected the main careers that they had seen in action in their neighborhoods, and I wondered, if they had been exposed to more lawyers, health care professionals, financial planners, accountants, etc., would they have wanted to pursue those careers instead? It made me even more passionate about sharing what I knew with them.

The girls who came to IWOAW were excited about their flights, and appreciative of the eye-opening world available to them. As popular as the first year was, the second year was even better! In 2014, we had about 400 girls attend—ten times more than the inaugural event—and we invited even more speakers, including fabulous role models like the first Latina military fighter pilot who graduated from the Air Force, Retired Lieutenant Col. Olga Custodio, and scientists from NASA. The day expanded into an informal mentorship program with a group of pilots, a controller, airport manager, an acrobatic pilot, and military personnel.

Even more amazing, in that same year, 2014, I was contacted and told I was to receive the prestigious Jefferson Award for Public Service for my efforts to introduce women to careers in aviation. I was amazed and honored. I soon learned I was the first private pilot to ever receive a Jefferson Award. To this day, it is one of my proudest (and most unexpected!) achievements.

Today, I am the co-president of a different group of amazing professionals, the Women of Aviation International San Francisco Bay Area Chapter, that is part of WAI (Women

In Aviation), without leaving my roots at IWOAW. I am also a Farmers Insurance Agent, but my passion for changing the conversation surrounding women in aviation remains as true as ever.

The lack of diversity in aviation, especially among women, needs to change, but before it does, we need to see more changes in the systems that affect women in aviation. What do I mean?

CREATING CHANGE

HIGH SCHOOLS. We must start at the base, meaning we must empower every girl out there to be part of a STEM class. Science, Technology, Engineering and Math are cool and powerful. It all starts with education and making it interesting for them is the key.

UNIVERSITIES. Before we can have diversity in the industry, we need to have diversity at the university level. Latinas are a large group in the country, but they still lag behind in numbers compared to other minorities when it comes to completing a college education. Colleges need to open doors and invite them into STEM programs that can put them on a career path for opportunities within aviation and aerospace.

NICHE AREAS. Few people realize that the people who fly drones are FAA-registered pilots. Think about it. To fly a five-pound drone above 400 feet takes the type of skill that a pilot has. Just like the pilot of a small plane, a drone pilot must understand the effects of air, weather, and terrain to fly a drone safely. Drones are an example of a niche area of aviation that few people, including Latinas, know about. Just think if they were introduced to the possibilities in high school.

NEW TECHNOLOGY AND THEIR OPPORTUNITIES. Companies like General Electric are continuing to build better motors for aviation, while new, better technology and tracking systems are making the job easier for air traffic controllers. Exposing young people to the new technologies in play can excite their imaginations and help them see the future, how it will affect aviation, and most importantly, how they can become a part of it.

In the tapestry of opportunities available in aviation, we need to weave in inspiration to those who can make a difference. My wish is that in five years, we will see women in every role within aviation. I would like to see more women owning aviation schools, aviation companies, and working in the upper management of the airlines. All these areas of the aviation industry are still dominated by males, but I have hope that with mentorship, and by giving young ladies experiences within aviation, that could change.

I tell every young lady I meet my motto: "Remember, the sky is not the limit; it is the beginning of the journey." I hope they believe me. Because if they do, I know I will see them excelling in the field of aviation someday!

Ana Uribe-Ruiz is an agent for Farmers Insurance and Co-President of Women in Aviation, San Francisco Bay Area Chapter. She can be contacted at: wai.sfba@gmail.com, at www.waisfbayarea. org or follow @WSfbayarea on Twitter or Facebook at Women in Aviation San Francisco Bay Area.

COVID-19 POSTSCRIPT

Here in California, where airspace is usually quite crowded and the air is usually tinged with smog, we are appreciating the positive effects of COVID-19. Because we own our own plane, we have no restrictions in flying. From several thousand feet above, we notice clearer air and greener foliage, a most likely result from the reduced commuter traffic now that we're all working from home. The sky seems bluer and the birds are happier. My husband feels like he is medicated for his asthma, but in actuality, his lungs are just being treated to cleaner air.

With commercial air traffic dramatically reduced, we've even had the opportunity to fly into some major airports, like San Jose and Oakland, to do a "touch and go" landing and takeoff. It's been a lot of fun to fly on the same runways used by much bigger, commercial planes!

On the downside, we can take flights, but can't really go anywhere when we land. Our son graduated from high school this year and could not attend a ceremony. He loves being at home and the quarantine has given us a lot of time to spend together, walking, painting, and going to virtual classes. We do our best to enjoy the moment.

But I started thinking about his generation and all they have endured in their lifetime. Born in the shadow of 9/11, they grew up in a world where in school they practiced shooter drills rather than fire drills. Now they have experienced the grip of a pandemic. Surely the survival of these experiences will create strong, excellent leaders for the future. One effect of COVID-19 may well be the creation of a generation that is stronger and more resilient than any who have come before.

LEARNING IT ALL

AMANDA GRACE COLÓN NUÑEZ

CURRENT POSITION
Aircraft Mechanic & Accident Investigator

FAVORITE AIRCRAFT
SR71 Blackbird
Used for NASA high-speed, high-altitude aeronautical research.
Hope to see one someday in a museum!

FAVORITE QUOTE
"Somewhere something incredible is waiting to be known."
–Carl Sagan

FUN FACT
I hope to someday go to Mars.

I was with my eighth-grade class in my hometown of Oswego, Illinois, outside of Chicago. I was on the school lawn, standing with toes just behind the safety line of a roped off area. It was a beautiful day in May. One of the major projects at the end of the year was to build and launch a cardboard rocket and now, after about two weeks of preparation, we were ready. The goal of the contest was not just to send your rocket up as high as possible, but to also load the rocket with a good parachute so it would have a long flight on the way down.

One by one, each group began shooting off their rockets into the air while my teacher started the stopwatch. Thud. Some made an almost immediate return to earth. Whoosh. Some had a brief and uneventful flight. My group's flight, however, was magical. My rocket shot up into the blue sky, expertly deployed the parachute and rode the air on the descent, logging the longest flight on the clock. It was then I realized that I wanted to know more about flight, rockets, and aerospace in general. And it was also validation that I could successfully build things, a talent that came completely naturally to me.

MISS FIX IT

I've always been a girl with a lot of interests, but early in life, my natural curiosity for taking things apart and fixing things emerged. I loved the challenge. It felt so satisfying!

I entered Oswego High School and decided to take as many advanced science and engineering classes as I could. My interests were numerous, but always came back to the "hands-on" aspect of actually repairing and building things myself. It seemed that for someone with my skills, who liked to take things apart just to see how they worked, engineering was a career I needed to consider! However, when looking at colleges, some engineering programs were definitely more academic than others. Did I just want some kind of maintenance program or an actual engineering degree? I knew I didn't want to stop working hands-on, fixing and building things. Then there was my interest in aerospace, rockets, and aviation. How did that all fit in? I wanted to study it all!

After an extensive search, I found a program close to home that brought all of these things together. It was the Aviation and Aerospace technology program at Lewis University in Romeoville, IL. Lewis combined aviation maintenance with a specialization in the aerospace industry that included some design and repair of propulsion and aerospace structures in addition to the mathematics, chemistry and physics required for more advanced aircraft and spacecraft maintenance. Perfect, I thought. Everything I wanted to study within one program. Finally, I could learn it all!

LESSONS AT LEWIS

I soon found I had chosen a difficult course of study with, at first, no mentors along the way to help. I was the first person in my family to attempt a career in aviation maintenance. My mom worked at a local community college and my dad was a district manager for a petroleum company. My older sister was already in college, studying journalism and Latino/Latina studies. So, although they were very proud and supportive of me, they could not give advice when it came to selecting classes for my major or succeeding in them.

I remember how daunting it was on the first day of school when the instructors went over all the work that we had to do in the lab throughout the course of the semester. For example, I had a course called Aircraft Structures 1, it was a course focused on sheet metal fabrication and repair. Sheet metal? I had built rockets out of cardboard, had never worked with sheet metal before let alone used a rivet gun to build a structure! I learned how to build parts of an airplane. There were times that fear of failure set in, but I soon learned that I just had to put the work in and ask for help when I needed it. I ended up getting an A in the class and lab, and even got assigned by my professor to help rebuild the ribs, skin and spar of a Cessna 150 wing that was dropped on the hangar floor.

I studied...a LOT. I had tests every week and I put more effort into college than I ever did in high school. My professors were there to help, and my family was cheering for me on the sidelines. How could I let them all down? Whenever I'd feel down, I would always tell myself, *this is what you love, this is your baby, what you love to do and what you are good at doing!*

I was glad that I had a leg up on aviation terminology, thanks to my part-time job, working at a small, nearby flight school where I took care of a lot of the administration. After my parents brought me there for a discovery flight when I was in high school, and I experienced the wonderful power of sitting in a plane and being at the controls, I knew I had to be involved in aviation in one way or another. I had read online that working at a flight school was a great way to get involved with aviation early, and it was. It was a great place to learn and help me earn my way through college.

Working there helped expose me to aviation terminology and give me access to people in the industry. While working there for about three years, I had also begun my flight training and soloed an aircraft, ironically, even before I could drive!

Being one of the only women in the program was a challenge. Before people really got to really know me, I had to endure comments from my male and even female classmates who had trouble accepting my sincere interest in aviation. I'd hear things like, "You wear too much makeup for a mechanic," "You don't really want to get your hands dirty, do you?" or the funniest comment of all, "You're just here for the boys, aren't you?" However, I always detected their jealousy and had talks with myself to keep going and refuse to let them make me feel less than them.

I've learned to deal with the mean comments and focus on my passion and goals. I've seen the change in them too. As they realized my passion and commitment for aviation, the comments stopped and I earned their respect, and a lot of new friends along with it.

INVESTIGATING THE INDUSTRY

Working at the flight school was rewarding, as that was my first real step into the industry, but as I kept progressing in school,

I realized that staying there all four years was not my heart's calling. I left to focus on school, and to find a job that allowed me to use all of the skills I obtained as an aviation maintenance major. Soon after, I landed an internship at DVI Aviation. The company was located nearby at a local airport and specialized in accident investigation, lab testing, material science, and aircraft maintenance. Their overall mission is to improve air safety, and we work on investigative cases in which there were aviation equipment failures or accidents.

The work combines all my interests—the hands-on mechanics of repair and reconstruction, a lot of lab research and chemical analysis, office research about different materials, aircraft and other cases etc. I've gotten to build engines, test fluids, use top of the line lab equipment, build electrical systems, and so much more. The work is incredible, fascinating, and definitely a possible career option after graduation. However, bigger dreams push me onwards and upwards.

The aerospace industry is an incredible place to be these days. I got to attend the 2020 Women in Aviation Conference in Orlando this year and at the same time I had the once-in-a-lifetime opportunity to attend the launch of SpaceX's Falcon 9 Rocket CRS-20. I remember standing on the beach, experiencing the dramatic countdown, then watching it blast into the sky, en route to deliver experiments and supplies to the international space station. It was truly amazing, and the first rocket launch I ever got to see in person. It took me back to the days of my eighth-grade class and captured my imagination. It reminded me of why I'm here and encouraged me to dream about what I can do within the industry.

It also reminded me of one of the most beautiful things about the aviation and aerospace industry and everyone in it: we all understand that we are working towards something that will forever be greater than ourselves. Faster, more high-performance and safer aircraft, rockets, and spacecraft landing on other worlds are all the stuff of dreams. It is an industry of exploration, and as we look to new worlds, the possibilities are nothing short of breathtaking.

My ultimate goal? I want to help send people to Mars, something that I'm hopeful will surely take place in our lifetime. Eventually working at NASA or SpaceX as an avionics or propulsion technician to contribute to the mission would be a dream come true. More school, experience, and time will be needed to accomplish this, but I'm prepared to do whatever it takes to get to my goal.

When you have got a passion, you can't help but do anything else but keep working towards your goal. A wonderful byproduct of doing this is inspiring other women with the same dreams and adventurous heart that I have. The future is one exciting treasure chest and I feel like I'm holding the key. All I have to do is keep learning and looking forward.

Amanda Grace Colón Nuñez is a sophomore at Lewis University and works as an aircraft mechanic and accident investigator at DVI Aviation. She can be reached at amandagracecolon@gmail.com or on Instagram @astronautamanda or Twitter @astro_amanda.

COVID-19 POSTSCRIPT

The 2020 Women in Aviation conference was held during my spring break at Lewis. I traveled to Florida with my mom and my boyfriend and that was when we found out that we wouldn't be back to Lewis for a long time. The country was shutting down state by state, school by school, store by store. Being in school full time, it always felt like the world was running at 100 mph. I would've never expected such an abrupt halt.

March would be the last time I'd step foot in my classes or the maintenance hangar at Lewis for a while. All of our classes were put on hold for another week, and we transferred to online learning. It was really difficult, but my professors are like my best friends, and they have always been there for all of the students.

As soon as the order is lifted, aviation majors will return to Lewis to make up all of the lab hours required of us by the FAA, while wearing masks and staying six feet apart. I'm interested to see how it'll work since some maintenance tasks cannot be performed by yourself if you want to do them safely. But, I'm optimistic and know that the aviation department is doing everything they can to control the situation while keeping everyone safe and healthy.

THE WIND BENEATH MY WINGS

DANIELA RAQUEL CARABAJAL

CURRENT POSITION
Corporate Pilot

FAVORITE AIRCRAFT
F4U Corsair and the Challenger 300
It's "my office" these days!

FAVORITE QUOTE
"Querer es poder." –Maria Carabajal (my mother)
("Where there is a will, there's a way.")

FUN FACT
I used to be a gymnast and hope to someday try aerobatics.

My father, Carlos Julio Carabajal, was a native of Montevideo, Uruguay, a town he loved. He loved aviation and earned his private pilot's license there at the age of sixteen. And he had a dream. Carlos wanted to come to the U.S., work there, and return to Uruguay in a Cessna 152. In fact, this dream was the reason he came to the U.S. in the first place! In a way, he only achieved both those dreams, and as he did, he served as the inspiration for everything that happened to me.

DAUGHTER PILOT

My father and my mother were both hardworking immigrants who held factory jobs. My mother, Maria, was from Mexico. They settled in a northern suburb outside of Chicago called Hoffman Estates. My father loved everything about aviation and would often take me, my mother, and my siblings to watch the planes take off at the nearby local airports, especially at the Schaumburg airport, which was closest to our house. We also saw any air show we could, and I remember how his eyes would light up as he would tell me about his experiences as a pilot flying in his home country of Uruguay. Here in the U.S., flying just seemed out of reach for him.

On Father's Day in 2005, while my mom was cooking a special dinner, my father and I took a quick trip to the Schaumburg airport to watch the airplanes take off and land. A flight instructor spotted us there and asked if I wanted to go up for a flight.

"Oh, that's ok, we're just looking," I replied, figuring the flight would be rather expensive.

"No, she'll do it," my father suddenly said, to my surprise. I guess he wanted me to experience the same joy he felt when he used to fly. The instructor told us to come back around six o'clock, so we returned home until it was time for the flight. I ran in the house excitedly and told my mom what I was going to do.

"She is not going up in a little plane like that just for fun!" mom said, obviously worried for my safety.

"Don't worry about it," my dad reassured her. "If she likes it, then you can worry!"

It turned out that dad had saved a little money to cover the cost of the flight, expecting me to enjoy flying as much as he did. And guess what? I did! It was time for my mom to worry because I absolutely knew I had to get back up in the air again!

By the time I was nineteen, my father knew I wanted to make flying a career. It was then he told me he had saved six thousand dollars and wanted to put it towards my private pilot's license. I was teaching gymnastics and attending Harper Community College, working on an associate degree, but I now added flight training three times a week to my busy schedule.

After I got my private pilot's license, I knew I didn't want to stop. I guess I had caught the same bug my father had. I needed to get my instrument rating next, and we agreed that it made sense to attend a college where I could pursue a career as a professional pilot. We settled on Aviator College of Aeronautics (AU) in Fort Pierce, Florida. My dad was so excited, but to attend, I needed a loan and getting a loan was difficult. Only my parents were able to apply for one, but their credit wouldn't qualify them. But when we finally saved enough to go, I remember how excited he was for me. His dream for me to become a pilot was coming true.

FOR DAD

My father was my long distance support every step of the way in my training. I spoke with him before and after almost every flight, sharing what I have learned, and telling him what was next in my journey. He offered advice, comfort, and moral support. Whenever I felt myself failing, he would buck me up and make me believe I could conquer the world. One time he sent me a recording of the song *Wind Beneath my Wings* by Bette Midler. No, I thought to myself, he is the wind beneath MY wings! I could always feel his presence with me and knew that together, I could complete the program with flying colors.

I had only been at AU about four months, but I was already deep into my training, when I received a sudden, unexpected call from home. It was my sister on the other end of the phone and I immediately knew something was wrong.

"Daniela," she began, with tears in her voice. "Dad had to have surgery on his aorta. It's an aneurism. He's still in surgery... but you should come home."

Immediately, the bottom seemed to drop out of my world as I stood in shock with the phone in my hand. My healthy, happy father who I had spoken to only the day before was in a life-threatening surgery.

I arrived in Chicago, rushed to the hospital, and found my family, gathered in the waiting room. To this day I can still see my brother's anxious face and my mother, standing there in tears, with a priest.

"I'm sorry, Daniela, he's gone."

Like a sudden rush, I could feel something leave me. As I stood in shock, my mother gently explained that they had found the aneurism, but he had died from complications of surgery. How could it be? My father was one of those people who had never even been ill. He was only sixty-six years old.

My plan was to stay in Chicago with my family. My father truly had been the wind beneath my wings and now, the uplift of his love and support was gone. I was on my own and had lost all interest in flying. How could I go on flying without knowing he was there, cheering me on?

Everyone at the flight school was very sympathetic, for they had met my father on several occasions, to assure him that I was in good hands. They encouraged me to finish my program if for no other reason than to honor my father. My mother and I, both shattered with grief for his loss, considered the same course of action.

"It is what he would have wanted," she said, but for me, I knew that going on without him would be so difficult. I needed to keep him in the forefront of my mind as my "why" for continuing my training. Just as she was that historic Father's Day, my mother was still nervous for me, but she trusted the program and supported me as much as she could to fill the void that my father's passing had left.

In 2009, I completed the professional pilot program at AU with a multi-private license, and multi-instrument, multi-commercial, single-commercial, multi-instrument instructor, instrument instructor and single-engine instructor ratings. The graduation party was bittersweet because the person who would have appreciated it the most was not there to see it.

I returned to Chicago and my plan was to become a flight instructor at a local flight school to get my hours. Then one day, I was approached by a family friend about a business associate they knew who was buying a private jet and looking for a pilot. He owned a very successful construction company and required weekly travel, mainly in the United States but to Central and South America as well. When we connected, he offered to put me through flight training to become the official pilot for his Citation VII series super-mid jet. I knew it as a beautiful, new, incredibly fast aircraft that held up to nine passengers. I immediately said yes!

After training and becoming type-rated for their aircraft, I was ready to go. It was my first aviation job and I must admit I was a little nervous, but I also knew that my dad would have been proud. As I immersed myself in becoming a corporate pilot, my goal of becoming a commercial airline pilot gradually faded away as I discovered the freedom and flexibility involved in flying for corporate operations.

I flew the corporate Citation VII for about two years and thoroughly enjoyed flying the company jet around the world. We flew to fun destinations in Argentina, Peru, Panama, and the Caribbean Islands. On longer trips, I stayed overnight and took some leisure time to sightsee and relax. I would pack a bag and sunbathe on the beach or ski in the mountains. It was heavenly!

FULL CIRCLE

I feel so lucky now. I wake up every morning and feel like I'm getting paid to do a hobby that I love. I've also come to appreciate the obvious differences between flying for commercial airlines versus corporate operations.

I love the autonomy of being a corporate pilot and I prefer the variety in routes, the flexible schedule, and the longer trips. I also like flying a smaller, lighter, much faster aircraft which cruises at forty-five thousand feet, about ten thousand higher than commercial aircraft; it's so much more efficient! I also enjoy the hands-on details involved in planning the corporate flights and attending to customer service for the passengers while on board. I concern myself with the aircraft itself, its cleanliness, catering, and special requests of the clients. For me, it's not just about flying from point A to point B but giving the passengers a memorable flight.

I still have never worked for the airlines. Corporate flights work with my lifestyle, and these days I fly a Challenger 300. I work closely with my flight deck partner to ensure safe and efficient operations and provide a collaborative environment where we can resolve any discrepancies. Through it all, my father is never far from my mind.

I remember one particular trip in the Citation to Argentina. I was thinking about my father and suddenly became very emotional when I realized how close we were to Uruguay, the home country he loved so much. I remembered his dream, and how he wanted to return there in a Cessna, to visit the people from his past, especially a friend of his named Marta.

Marta and my father were very close while growing up in the same neighborhood. My father's parents and Marta's parents were friends, so they were like brother and sister. However, through the years, they had fallen out of touch.

Then, about a year after my father passed, my brother Carlos had some interesting news for me. Marta's daughter had reached out to my family through social media. She found Carlos, who gave her the bad news that my father had passed. I suddenly felt a strong pull on my heartstrings to connect with Marta and her daughter. Surely, it would be what my father would want me to do. Maybe he couldn't fulfill his dream of returning to his home country in a Cessna, but I could do it for him!

I was amazed when I connected back to Marta and she told me she was now living in Argentina and would love to meet me. On one of the Cessna's trips to Buenos Aires, we arranged to meet at the Four Seasons Hotel. As I walked to the appointed place, I recognized Marta from her Facebook photo. When we saw each other, we hugged like old, long-lost friends. She had been familiar to me from my father's stories for so long that I felt like I had known her all my life.

Here was someone who remembered my father as a pilot. And, she almost immediately recognized how my father and I were such kindred spirits. Her eyes sparkled as she took a good look at me.

"He always said he would return in a Cessna," she said, "and he has." We both teared up as we remembered his joy and love of aviation. I felt somehow that I had come full circle with my father. He had helped me achieve my dream, and I had helped him achieve his.

A few years later, my mother arranged to carry out one of my father's final wishes. Our family returned to the town he loved, Montevideo, Uruguay, for a special memorial service to scatter his ashes there, surrounded by those who remembered him. It was a fitting tribute for a man with a dream who was the wind beneath my wings that gave me life, love, and the inspiration to fly.

Daniela Raquel Carabajal is a professional corporate pilot of a Challenger 300, based out of New York. She can be reached at Daniela.Raquel1@gmail.com.

COVID-19 POSTCRIPT

Although I am based in New York, which has been hit so hard by the pandemic, I am fortunate in that I fly a corporate jet for an owner and am onboard with the same handful of people I've always flown. As their mobility has decreased, so has my flight time, and we are definitely staying in the country. For other charter companies, who have flights to fill in order to make a profit, COVID has been devastating. Aircraft are expensive to maintain and must be maintained whether or not they are in use.

Just like all aircraft these days, we are taking extra precautions with cleaning before and after every flight but of course, since fewer people are in the airplane to begin with, it's a safer environment than others. Here in New York, the date to lift the quarantine has been pushed back to June, and we don't know what will happen after that. I'm just grateful I can continue flying, even on a limited basis, as we all battle this virus.

ONE CHALLENGE AT A TIME

ANA PAULA GOMEZ PUERTO

CURRENT POSITION
First Officer, Copa Airlines

FAVORITE AIRCRAFT
Aerobus 380
I hope to fly one to longer routes one day.

FAVORITE QUOTE
Rely on faith.

FUN FACT
I am the only Mexican woman pilot at Copa.
The air traffic controllers know me by my accent!

"Is becoming an airline pilot difficult?"

I've been asked this question many times, and I know many other airline pilots have been asked it as well. And if you ask ten pilots that question, you'd get ten different answers. If you ask me, I'd have to reply that it is definitely "challenging."

But when you have your first discovery flight in a new, beautiful country, with a funny instructor who is determined to thrill you, how can you walk away without wanting more? My first flight was on August 6, 2014, in Panama in a Cessna 172 with an instructor who called me *"taquito"* because I was Mexican. He told me not to be any more afraid than I would be on a passenger plane. Over the Lake of Calzada Larga, which is an area where many pilots practice their flying in Panama, he asked me if I was scared, but I was mainly excited. I felt like we were almost touching the water as we zipped and zoomed just over the lake. My adrenaline rose and I had that "roller coaster" feeling as I laughed in joy at the feelings within me. Yes, I wanted to become a pilot, just like my father. At least that's what I thought at the time.

NEW CHALLENGES

I grew up in the beautiful, coastal state of Quintana Roo in Mexico, although my parents tell me that when I was one or two years old, we did live in Verona, Italy for a time. I was the third of four children and have a younger sister as well as an older and younger brother. I attended school in Monterrey and my father supported the family working as a mechanic. However, he always had a dream to become a pilot. It took him years, but, eventually, he went through all the groundwork and flight training to become a commercial pilot. He earned his certification and found a position at a Mexican airline called Aviacsa. A few years later, when the airline went bankrupt, my father started looking for work elsewhere.

That's how the family ended up in Panama, with my father taking a job with Copa Airlines, the largest airline in Panama. I was thirteen when we moved to the country, and at first, I just couldn't get used to it. I missed my friends and activities back in Mexico, even though Panama seemed like a safer, more modern, and more closely-knit community. Everybody seemed to know everybody else. Panama is so much smaller than the expansive land of Mexico, where there is a wide variety of topography, weather, and population depending on where you are. Panama is much more compact and seems to have two seasons—sunny and hot, or rainy. It reminds me a bit of Cancun, Mexico.

It also seemed like everyone in Panama spoke English, which I did not learn well while living in Mexico. This became one of my most immediate challenges. Giving speeches in school was difficult and many times the students laughed at me for speaking English improperly or speaking Spanish with a Mexican accent.

By the time I graduated high school I felt a lot better about both my new home country and speaking English. I was still interested in becoming a pilot but began to doubt myself. Sure, everyone likes aviation in the moment, but maybe I wouldn't like it as a career. How do I know I'd be good at it? Maybe I wasn't cut out to be a pilot. My father encouraged me but didn't push me. He has always let me be independent and study and make decisions on my own. So, I had to decide if I was ready to embark upon the adventure of becoming a pilot all by myself. It took a few months, but finally I decided to take the plunge.

The next challenge was financial. Flight school was expensive and when I enrolled in 2014, we depleted my savings and enough of my family's money to make it happen. Then, as a solution, I transferred to a different flight school that offered scholarships for half tuition. To enter the school and try to get the scholarship, I had to do well on a test. So, I took the test the first time but didn't qualify for the scholarship or admission. I took the test again, and once again failed. I felt the pressure on many levels because I just had three opportunities to be admitted. The third time I took the test, I was admitted to the school! I was very glad, but it was just the beginning of my journey to get that scholarship. I had to study very hard in school and as I progressed through the years, it was harder and harder on my family to keep me going.

One day my dad told me that in order for me to complete my training they would have to sell the house in Cancun. It was a difficult decision, but I thought that perhaps I could get through the program before the house actually sold. I already had four years into the program that was to take only eighteen months, and I was determined to finish as quickly as possible. Once again, I took the scholarship exam and this time, like a miracle, I earned the exact amount of money I needed to complete my education! I may not have been the best student, but I was most in need. Other students could get a loan but because I was not considered a Panamanian citizen, or someone who had permanent residency with ten years living in the country, I could not get one. A scholarship was the only way I could have paid my way through school. I was so excited and grateful, but the challenges weren't over.

My father was doing well as a pilot at Copa, but the idea of working at the same company as my father both scared me a little and made me feel excited, too.

First of all, I would be a new pilot at a very established, well-respected airline. What if I wasn't good enough? I had heard there was a lot of competition in that airline, that I would have to work harder and be better. If I failed, everyone would know, including the people who worked with my dad, which would be terrible. Was it worth the risk?

But it was time for the next challenge. I applied and was hired by Copa airlines, then placed in training to receive my Boeing 737 rating. I was impressed by my fellow pilots and couldn't help but compare myself to them. All too often, I was sure they were better than me, or advancing faster than me. It may or may not have been the case, but unfortunately, it was what I sometimes told myself.

In the end, I overcame all of my challenges. I completed the program and took my place as a First Officer on the airline's Boeing 737, where I have served for almost two years.

GOOD ENOUGH

Through reflection, I've since learned that the journey to pilot has been a unique learning experience, not only in aviation, but in how to become my own supporter. Looking back on my life, I see many times I thought I couldn't do something but went ahead and was completely successful in the end. There were times I worried, or thought people doubted me when it was actually me who had the doubt all along. Now I know that determination and faith are the most important tools to get us to a place where we are confident and our own cheerleaders in any situation.

Years later, in conversations with other captains and pilots, I have learned that others have also felt like I did at times—like they weren't good enough or everyone was waiting for them to fail. Truthfully, Copa has been an encouraging place to work where everyone works as a team to help others succeed.

Sometimes I step into the cockpit and have to work with someone I don't know. Where once I would worry about what that person thought of me, today I know that I have to stay positive about interactions. It's important to take the good advice and put aside the bad vibes that may be coming from the person next to you, because we all have bad days in our life and sometimes it's difficult to be positive all the time. However, we must be respectful. If you aren't careful, the words and actions of negative people can sink you into a place of insecurity where you don't belong. I've learned to make the best out of every flying experience, with every captain. You have to leave everything else aside. Most of the time you'll build a good friendship with the captain, and sometimes not, but it doesn't matter because you are there to fly.

Sometimes I step into the cockpit and I'm flying with another woman. I'm lucky that Copa actually has hundreds of female pilots and it fills me with pride when I'm assisting a female captain. It gives me hope for my future, that I may soon be sitting in that seat myself, and it makes me feel part of an even bigger team—of female commercial airline pilots around the world. In the meantime, I just try to enjoy it when someone (usually a man) mistakes me for an airport assistant. It will probably take years before nobody is surprised that their airplane has a female captain.

Then, sometimes there are the best, most wonderful days when I walk into the cockpit and my dad is sitting in the captain's seat. Usually they are planned, but sometimes they are still a surprise. Those days fill him with pride while they fill me with joy and gratitude to be able to share something so special with him. Our first flight together was to Cordoba, Argentina with our family onboard. It was a memorable milestone! Now, as we stand at the front of the plane, greeting the passengers as they board or deplane, we have been asked if we are related. It always results in a happy photo opportunity when we reveal ourselves to be father and daughter.

CHALLENGES PRESENT AND FUTURE

Have my challenges ended? Absolutely not. Every flight comes with new and different ones. The everchanging weather in Panama is always a challenge, as is planning flights. Part of staying a good pilot is never to get too comfortable. I'm always challenging myself to be a better pilot because there are changing variables for every flight, from airspace requirements, to national emergencies, to airports, to weather. I always welcome the unusual landings through the swirling Gulf winds of Cancun or the blustery, desert gusts of Las Vegas.

Getting where I am has been a series of challenges, faced one at a time. Along the way, there were things in my control and out of my control, but the important thing I've done is to remain faithful to goals and never give up. Oh, and remember, too, that sometimes, when challenges seem too difficult, you may be blocking yourself. A change in attitude may be exactly what you need.

Paula Gomez is a First Officer for Copa Airlines in Panama. She can be reached at paulagmzpto@gmail.com, aviacionconpaulita. com, and on Instagram @aviacionconpaulita.

COVID-19 POSTSCRIPT

It's a difficult time for everyone in the industry and like many airline pilots, I am not flying at all these days. My last flight was March 19, from Panama to Cancun and back to Panama, and in the meantime, I have decided to leave the company. Copa has helped me a lot and one day I hope to return, but God knows what will happen. In the meantime, I am preparing myself for my next challenge, even as I weather COVID-19, which is the biggest challenge for all of us.

I am using the extra time to connect with others online and educate myself. Since I am always working to improve my English, I am in an English course that is specifically for pilots so that is a lot of fun. I'm also taking an online class in economics and finance, and of course, taking time to cook from scratch and watch movies. I am also preparing to return to my native country, Mexico, after eleven years here in Panama. I will leave behind a part of myself and I hope to one day return but God only knows what is in store for me and my boyfriend, who keeps me from giving up and is always there to support me. I am glad I have such a good partner!

One thing I am sure about—everything in the future will be better than it is right now.

CASTALIA SERNA

CURRENT POSITION
Deputy Commissioner, Concessions & Customer Service

FAVORITE AIRCRAFT
Boeing 747. My husband is from France and it always took me comfortably across the Atlantic to see him when we were dating.

FAVORITE QUOTE:
"Challenges bring opportunities."

FUN FACT
Growing up, I was always the oddball.

You can't grow up in Chicago without knowing our two great airports. First, there is the small yet bustling Midway airport, which is located eight miles outside the city. It was Chicago's primary airline hub until the mighty O' Hare International was built in 1955. O'Hare consistently ranks among the world's busiest airports and if you have ever been there, you understand why.

RUNWAY DREAMS

When I was younger, I used to dream of working at the airport. I did not know how it was going to happen, but my love of foreign languages made me think about the thousands of people who came through the airport in one day, and how our worlds might someday intersect.

My family was from Mexico and I grew up on the West Side of Chicago. At home, we spoke Spanish. In school, I studied French. I also studied Italian, Greek, and Indonesian along the way. But after attending the University of Illinois at Chicago, my dream came true when I took my first job in the airline industry. Additionally, I started a position with the City of Chicago, Department of Aviation as a customer service representative in the 1990's. For the job, it was mandatory to speak two languages besides English, so I was all set.

After a time in customer service, I had the opportunity to branch into public relations at the airport. However, I left in 2006 to help the City of Chicago in different government agencies. My responsibilities and knowledge grew with each career move. First, I worked in the Department of Planning and Development and then as community relations manager for the Cook County Department of Corrections. I went on to work as the Director of External Affairs and as a Director with the Illinois State Comptroller. In each position I learned how to deal with government agencies, including the FBI, as I took on an increasing number of complex and challenging government roles. In 2018, I returned to the Chicago Department of Aviation (CDA) to assume my current position as Deputy Commissioner, Concessions & Customer Service for the CDA airports. It was then that I felt I was "home" and had come full circle in my career.

I also felt more ready and prepared for the challenging position I was about to undertake. By leaving the airport and having other experiences working in government, I returned having earned my stripes. All the previous challenging experiences had prepared me well for my new ones in this position. I tell the Latinas I mentor the same thing. All of our experiences can lead you somewhere new and different, so appreciate what you can about your entry-level jobs. They may help you get a leg up someday!

DEPUTY DUTY

As Deputy Commissioner, my job is busy, exciting, and certainly never boring. I feel blessed for the work. I oversee the concessions and customer service experience for both Midway and O'Hare guests. I feel as if airports are the new malls. We have a diverse, captive audience and it is up to us to offer amenities that make them want to return the next time they fly. For example, there are businesspeople on layovers who need special services and conveniences. Families particularly with small children need diversions, like a fun or relaxing family lounge. There are people with dietary restrictions who require suitable dining options.

I feel we serve all travelers by anticipating their needs. I am directly involved in obtaining the best quality food and beverages which we provide, as well as planning for the optimal use of public spaces at both airports.

My position also serves a significant public relations capacity. I am engaged in special events at the airport and exciting marketing initiatives as well. When anything is filmed at O'Hare, I have an integral role in the logistics and coordination of our entire team to ensure everything runs smoothly.

During my years in the sheriff's office, I worked closely with human trafficking victims. Today, I once again have the opportunity to assist in building awareness of this problem by working on a human trafficking awareness campaign at both CDA airports. This is in conjunction with Mayor Lori Lightfoot's office, the Illinois Department of Human Services, and in partnership with the airline industry. I am honored and humbled to be helping address this serious global issue. I believe we have a responsibility to assist victims who do not have a voice and provide guidance so they can receive proper assistance. We also need to have open and consistent conversations with our children and others in general about the warning signs. It is my hope that our campaign will contribute to people becoming more informed about the issue, and perhaps even proactive in ending such human exploitation.

In anything I do, I never take all the credit or claim to achieve it alone. I would not be here without my parents, who were always supportive of my desire to pursue a career in aviation.

I also owe thanks to my wonderful daughter and husband who cooked many a dinner for themselves, as they had no choice but to tolerate my erratic work schedule. I also have an extraordinary team, and was lucky to have great mentors, like Jamie Rhee, the Commissioner of the Chicago Department of Aviation, to help me along in helping me find my passion. As I look back, I am also glad I "started at the bottom" in customer service, because it was there that I developed a hunger to become a bigger part of aviation in a very unique way. I am grateful for those experiences and try to always be a positive role model by being kind and courteous to everyone I encounter at the airports.

AVIATION INSPIRATION

As a Latina, I attend many meetings where I am one of a handful of women, and often the only woman who looks like I do. It does not matter though, because I know I have a mission to represent my community in a positive way. It makes me proud to be part of a living, breathing organization and even more proud when I can talk to other younger Latinas about what I do. Seeing their eyes light up as I describe my role is greatly rewarding.

When people think about jobs in aviation, they usually think of pilots and planes, but there is so much more to creating the aviation industry ecosystem that keeps our country on the move. Airports are an integral part of that and there are plenty of opportunities available to creative, diligent individuals willing to think out of the box.

Looking ahead to the future of our beloved Chicago airports,

I am excited that Midway now has twenty-five concessions. We are looking forward to boosting that to seventy-two retail, and specialty food and beverage outlets soon. I am also looking forward to the completion of the recent $8.5 billion expansion of O'Hare. The expansion includes a new runway, which will provide a more efficient structure as well as gate expansions. Even without the improvements, we have managed to cut flight delays from ten years ago, which makes us very proud.

Sometimes it is amazing for me to think that the big airports I once beheld as a little girl from afar are now like my "extended family members" that I help take care of everyday. It is a testament to where a vivid dream, hard work, experience, and a sprinkle of strong determination can get you.

Castalia Serna is Deputy Commissioner, Concessions and Customer Service at the Chicago Department of Aviation. Contact her at: castalia.serna2@cityofchicago.org

COVID-19 POSTSCRIPT

One of the most challenging times I have experienced in the airport industry, apart from 9/11, was the COVID-19 situation. Universally, it caught all of us by surprise but in the airport world, it really threw us for a loop.

I am a true believer that challenges bring opportunities to us. As we were dealing with the situation at hand, closing some of our amenities and concessionaires, we were also strategizing on our welcome back campaign to reintroduce ourselves back to our traveling guests. The silver lining is that it gives us the opportunity to get creative and embrace our team's efforts more than ever.

THE POWER OF WANDERLUST

YASMINE ABU ARAB

CURRENT POSITION
Flight Instructor at ATP

FAVORITE AIRCRAFT
Northrop Grumman B-2 Spirit

FAVORITE QUOTE
"There's more to life than being a passenger." - Amelia Earhart

FUN FACT
My bucket list goal is to take acrobatic flying lessons.

Some people take all their lives to figure out what they want to do. I guess I was lucky because I always knew I wanted to fly, even before I knew what flying was! Even as a child, I had a bad case of "wanderlust." I was interested in faraway places and wanted to visit them all. And perhaps the reason why I was so interested in other cultures of the world is because I grew up with an interesting mix of two of them within my very own home.

INTERCULTURAL INFLUENCE

My parents met as immigrants, taking an English class at a community college in their newly adopted home country, the United States. My mom was from Mexico and had moved here to live with her sister. My dad was from Israel and had been brought to the country by his job. Their cultures were polar opposites, and growing up in the Chicago area, I saw two very different worlds. It made me curious about what else was out there for me to discover.

I loved to travel but didn't get the opportunity as often as I would've liked. I did accompany my mother to Mexico a few times but never made it to Israel with my father. Each time I traveled, the desire to continue traveling grew. I was fascinated with all the different countries and cultures in the world and wanted to experience them all! As I got older, I began to see flying as part of the plan.

The trouble was, I didn't know anyone in aviation among my family or friends. I felt like it was all up to me, and I knew if I really wanted it, I would have to work really hard. I was in middle school when I secretly decided that somehow, someway, I was going to learn to fly. Then in high school, I had the opportunity to take an exploratory course on aviation that included private pilot ground school coursework. As a culmination of all we had learned, we took a field trip to the DuPage Airport and went up with a pilot for a 30-minute discovery flight. That was it for me. I knew what my plan was after school. I was going to be a pilot!

When I told my parents, they didn't believe me at first. They didn't speak out against it; they just didn't believe I would ever stick with it. My mom thought it was a wild, exciting idea and a great dream. My dad warned it would be difficult to raise a family or have a more traditional lifestyle. Both of them thought it was an attainable dream, but I would have to work hard and stick with it to really reach my goals. By the time I had expressed to them how committed and passionate I was about the decision, they understood. I felt like it was my destiny, and they were starting to see it too.

OSU

I looked for a bigger school that could offer me opportunities within aviation and I found it with The Ohio State University's aviation studies program, which is housed within their College of Engineering. I was expected to take some engineering classes but also receive flight training. The aviation requirements were actually equivalent to a minor area of study. If you didn't finish the flight training in time, it wouldn't hinder your degree, but my plan was to complete my flight training and obtain my pilot certificates from OSU in four years.

Although I never felt like being a Latina or a woman really held me back, I definitely felt in the minority. OSU was only four percent demographically Latino, and I was among only a handful of women in the aviation studies program. I took all the prerequisite courses and then began working on my flight training. Unfortunately, my progress towards my pilot's license ended up taking longer than that because whenever I returned home for breaks, it interrupted my training. I would return and often have to relearn things again. It was necessary, but frustrating as it delayed my progress.

I did however have a chance to compete in a thrilling aviation race representing the OSU Women in Aviation group in 2018. I was the treasurer of the OSU Women in Aviation group and had heard about a 100-year-old aviation race for women known as the Air Race Classic. It was a historic event that even Amelia Earhart had participated in. The year we competed it was a four-day, 2,656 mile race from Sweetwater, Texas to Fryeburg, Maine. The race was a kind of rally in which teams compete against each other based on their own predictions to different points, taking into account time, weather, performance, and gas mileage. I wondered why Ohio State had never entered a team before, but when I looked into the rules, I didn't see anything that would disqualify a team like ours. So, we approached the administration and they were all for it...provided we raised the money needed to make it happen all on our own!

Our whole Women in Aviation chapter spent over a year raising thousands of dollars to cover the cost of the entry fees for each person, for travel, lodging and aircraft transportation and fuel. We began by reaching out to regional airlines and many of them stepped up to sponsor us. We also asked companies that were based at an airport or had ties to the aviation department like flight service and fuel providers and airport diners. The OSU alumni were some of our most ardent supporters. We owe a debt of gratitude to those alumni who pledged even a modest amount like $25. We also received a donation from the College of

Engineering Priority Fund. We were so excited when we finally raised enough money to compete.

At the race, we could feel the high hopes of our supporters. We didn't want to let them down. The weather was clear, and all our plans were made. Once in the air, I thought flying the race felt differently from any of my other flights. The race tested our piloting skills and aviation decision making and I loved how dynamically I could fly to gain time in the air. When you're studying for your ratings, they teach you about different terrains and what different altitudes feel like but actually experiencing all of that taught me so much more than studying it in books or watching videos. It was a fast-paced, adventurous ride that kept me and my teammates on our toes the entire time!

I really enjoyed flying our route and it spoke to that curious part of me that likes to see new places. The Midwest is very flat and unchanging; you see basically nothing but cornfields, and then suddenly we were flying over mountains, hills and inland lakes of the south and then the northeastern seaboard. I was able to put some of the things I'd studied in books into action and cement my knowledge of a concept with real life experience. As I was racing, I could feel myself becoming a better pilot.

Our goal in finishing was to land in the top 10. When we crossed the finish line, we soon found out that our team, the "Lady Buckeyes," finished seventh out of 55 teams and second among collegiate teams. We were so proud of ourselves and happy that we had done well for all of those who had believed in us and supported us. I'm also proud that the Air Race Classic Team at

OSU continues and will probably be attending another race in the future. Starting the race team and affecting women's aviation at OSU was a shining moment in my college career!

AT ATP

Senior year, I had the choice of graduating in four years or staying longer and finishing up my flight training. I decided to finish my degree, graduate, and complete my flight training at the ATP Flight School in West Chicago.

ATP focused on fast-tracking flight training to get people into the airlines as soon as possible. Courses were intense and fast-paced, but I was ready. I was "all in" on aviation, so immediately after graduation, I powered through the rest of the ratings. I had already obtained a private pilot certificate at OSU but now I received six more ratings including instrument, commercial Single-Engine, Commercial Multiengine, CFI (Certified Flight Instructor), CFII (Certified Flight Instructor - Instrument), and MEI (Multiengine Instructor). After receiving my ratings, I was able to learn even more about aviation in greater depth while teaching it.

Today, I'm a flight instructor at DuPage Airport, working on getting the 1,500 flying hours I need to move towards my goal. I love the fast pace and variety of flying experiences that I get. I have students who are new to flying and soloing for the first time and those who are working towards becoming instructors too. It's been a challenge, and I've enjoyed figuring out the best techniques to work with others.

As Chicago and its suburbs are virtual melting pots, I've also enjoyed meeting many different types of people from different cultures. My Spanish has come in handy. I've discovered that I'm not alone in making sacrifices to pursue a passion to fly; my students do as well. I enjoy sharing my love for flying with them all and appreciate the opportunity to learn and become a better pilot on my way to my ultimate goal.

My wanderlust is still not satisfied. I've been to a few islands and had the great experience of studying abroad in South Korea. I chose South Korea because of its completely different culture, so I could learn both inside and outside the classroom. Now, Dubai tops my list as somewhere I'd most like to go.

I know I've been lucky, having the support of my now-believing parents who helped me get where I am today. I tell my two younger sisters, from my firsthand experience, that they can be anything they want to be. I like to speak to other young girls about the industry too because it breaks my heart to think of them limiting themselves because they have never seen a Latina in aviation or even another female doing what they may aspire to do. This is why I joined things like Women in Aviation and the Air Race Classic, and I highly recommend that all aspiring women pilots consider doing the same. The women I meet there are huge inspirations to me, and I hope one day I can do the same for someone else.

My parents have yet to fly with me, and I can't wait for the day I'm in the cockpit of a commercial airliner and they're sitting in first class. I love that they never said flying was too crazy a dream to reach. And I love that they were right.

Yasmine Abu Arab is a flight instructor and aspiring airline pilot at ATP. Reach her at yasabu@yahoo.com.

COVID-19 POSTSCRIPT

Recently, the global pandemic that we've been facing due to COVID has started to slow down the aviation industry. At first it was terrifying to think that the dream I've been working toward, that finally felt so close, could be ripped away. It has always been my ultimate career goal to be an airline pilot and that will continue to be a top priority for me in the following months and years. However, the pandemic has changed my timeline and expectations for my future. I am quickly approaching my 1500 hours and I expected to have an airline job lined up when I finished because that's how great the industry was when I started my training. Unfortunately, that's no longer the case and I'm not sure where my path will take me next.

I know I will continue aiming for the airlines, but my path will most likely not be as direct. I may take a few detours and venture out into different sides of aviation. I have no idea how long it'll take any more and that uncertainty is definitely nerve-racking, but I have tried to remain positive and look at the bright side of things. I fell in love with aviation because it's an incredible field and I am hopeful that it can bounce back. I plan on taking this as an opportunity to explore different types of flying and hopefully, renewing that passion for flying in other ways.

MELISSA MONTIEL JIMENEZ

CURRENT POSITION
First Officer

FAVORITE AIRCRAFT
Boeing 777–such a classic design!

FAVORITE QUOTE:
"When everything seems to be going against you, remember that the airplane takes off against the wind, not with it."

FUN FACT
I'm a pilot that's afraid of heights and thinks skydiving is completely illogical. Fly the airplane, don't jump out of it!

I was born and raised in the border town of Tijuana, Mexico, in a family with a history of strong women. My mom had chosen to become one of the first female doctors in her city, and struggled in a field that that was male-dominated at the time. Not only did she work in the emergency room, but she is now in business for herself as an entrepreneur. My grandmother had been fascinated with all things aviation. She owns a local radio station and used to host a talk show where she would feature topics such as what a regular day in the life of a pilot was like. Also, she would interview people in the industry and I was fascinated by her stories. We began sharing the same passion and got the whole family involved in making treks to San Diego to see the Blue Angels and other aviators perform at the airshows at the Miramar Air Force Base. I remember watching them do amazing maneuvers and they inspired me to think, "I can see myself in the world of aviation."

JOURNEY TO MEXICAN PILOT

I remember I was at San Diego State University, studying marketing when I began to feel a pull towards a career in aviation. I had always been fascinated with planes and loved going to big airports. I'd always see the airplanes and wonder where they were headed, and who was taking them there. Truthfully, though, I knew that I liked airplanes, but didn't know anything about flying. So, I booked an introductory class where they taught me the basics.

I will never forget that day. As Leonardo da Vinci said, "Once you have tasted flight, you will forever walk the earth with your eyes turned skyward. For there you have been, and there you will always long to return." That day I felt all the adrenaline of having operated an airplane. By the time I was listening to air traffic control and we were preparing the plane for landing, I was sold on a career in aviation. A plan formed in my mind, and soon I was excited to begin flight training. Unfortunately, though, I had trouble finding support for my plan.

Some people asked me if I were just doing it to find a husband. Others, like my family, told me it wasn't a real career. They thought of it as a hobby, and an expensive one too, so why would I go through all the trouble? They asked what I was rebelling against. I understood that these comments were coming from a place of fear.

I started to interview and talk to anyone I could about pursuing a career in aviation and what it took to make it happen. I also researched the number of women pilots out there—only five percent! But that was enough for me to know it could be done!

I decided to begin flight training in San Diego at an aviation school that had been recommended to me by several people.

I worked hard and pursued my ratings. Although my family was concerned at the beginning, once they saw how committed I was, they gave me their full support. Years later, once I finished all the training, I converted my license to ICAO in Mexico City and that is when my professional career started.

My first position was flying an Airbus 320 for an airline in Mexico. I was there from 2014-17. In my first year, a colleague told me that because I was a woman, I would have to prove myself and work twice as hard as a man. I was confused by that thought, but I understood where they were coming from. I have seen throughout my career, that we all work the same and they wanted me to take the position seriously, letting me know that I wouldn't have any special privilege. So, the thought of working as hard as a man was already something in me. After all, every pilot took the same test whether they were male or female. Sometimes I do have to confess that I felt disappointed that the world didn't see it that way. I thought the hardest part would be getting into the airlines, but little did I know that the first year of my job as an airline pilot would be the hardest, I would ever have.

One time, I had a passenger that refused to fly on my aircraft because he didn't feel safe with a female flying the airplane. But aviation is all about teamwork. As a team, we can't try to solve everything as a single pilot. We are taught to know how to communicate an issue and as a team, we work on solving an issue; negative attitudes can be detrimental to the process.

Everything is about attitude; if you are having a bad day, you have to learn what the problem was, let go of it, and learn from your mistake and prepare better next time. That is the most valuable thing I learned that year and will take with me for the rest of my career.

AMERICAN AVIATION

I was grateful when I got a position with an airline in the U.S. I couldn't believe my eyes when I walked into the new hire class and there were five other women there! I had never seen anything like it before. I realized in the U.S. there was more diversity, and therefore, more acceptance of female pilots too. I enjoyed having other women who could empathize with me. We exchanged similar stories and I found I was not alone in some of my experiences.

The wonderful thing about aviation is that no matter your race or sex, the plane is flown by the same rules. I'm also proud to be a work in progress. I take any feedback from anyone to become a better pilot as I continue my journey to captain. I can't wait to see what growth opportunities will come my way. I want to hold the standard of the Latina pilot very high, as we are known as hard workers, and that includes pilots too. We have an amazing culture and we are also team-oriented and very compassionate to others.

The best part of being a Latina in aviation is that it means I'm opening doors to a lot of other Latinos in this field. I show that what once seemed impossible, is very possible. As I am performing my duties as a pilot, I never know who I am inspiring. Often, pilots have told me that I am not just the first woman they've flown with, but also the first Mexican. I want to represent women and Latinas well, so I do my job impeccably with a high level of professionalism, but also the warmth and friendliness we are known for.

Aviation has not been just a career for me, but a lifestyle. It has not been easy to get to where I am, and I still have a long way to go. However, it has taught me how to work hard to accomplish my goals. Aviation has changed my life for the better. Since I started my career, I have had to give it one hundred percent effort, surround myself with people involved in aviation, and exercise the discipline needed to succeed in the field.

WHAT TO EXPECT

To those aspiring Latina pilots out there, I would offer the following advice: wanting to fly airplanes isn't enough. You need to persevere and believe in yourself.

For me, the journey was long, and because not everyone believed in me from the start, I had to believe in myself even more strongly. There will be many exciting days and also many obstacles, but you don't fail until you stop trying.

You will use this perseverance throughout your career in aviation. Things do not always go as planned. Pilots must be able to change gears quickly and move on to focus on how to solve an issue.

Being an airline pilot is a very exciting career, filled with fun and adventure. The amazing views you'll have from the cockpit, the trips, being in charge of the aircraft, and taking off and landing the airplane still gives me a sensation of exhilaration and an adrenaline rush. You'll visit so many cities and meet amazing people.

I also advise you to always be kind to everyone; you never know how life will make turns, so it is good to be on good terms with as many people as possible. Have a good attitude and always keep studying. In every field there will always be positive and negative people, but you have the control over how you react, and where you want to go in life.

Yes, aviation is a wonderful career, but remember to prioritize your needs. Know when you need to take a break and relax, make time for yourself, spend time with family or with a group of good, quality friends. Keep your loved ones close to you. Their support will make the journey lighter.

Melissa Montiel Jimenez is a First Officer. She can be reached on Instagram @flyme10.

COVID-19 POSTSCRIPT

As pilots, we are directly affected in economic recessions and other global crises.

All over the world, aviation has paused, and we will see some airlines go into bankruptcy. I believe it's a good idea for any aspiring pilot to have an economic backup plan in case things don't go well, just as pilots regularly prepare for possible, but unlikely scenarios in flight.

I know aviation will not disappear, but it will just take time to get back to how it was. Still, I'm proud to be part of an essential industry and help people continue to fly.

A WARRIOR'S SPIRIT

LINDA PFEIFFER PAUWELS

CURRENT POSITION
American Airlines Boeing 787 Captain & Check Airman

FAVORITE AIRCRAFT
Boeing 787
The way it feels when it flies is incredible.

FAVORITE QUOTE
"Dolium volvitur: An empty cask is easily rolled."

FUN FACT
In addition to English, I am fluent in French and Spanish, and studied Sanskrit.

My paternal grandfather died just before I was born, but I know his spirit lives within me.

His name was Franciszek Edward Pfeiffer. At first, all I

knew was that he was an officer in the Polish army during the Warsaw Uprising. Unfortunately, I never got to meet him, as he died before I was born. I didn't get to hear many stories either, because my own father died of an apparent heart attack at age 39, when I was six. Later, my brother Walter, who is also a pilot, learned more about our grandfather's lengthy military record after a few visits to the Polish Institute in London. Brigadier General Pfeiffer commanded the longest fighting unit during the Uprising and was awarded the Virtuti Militari, Poland's highest decoration for valor. He was a scholar as well, and worked extensively with youth, out of concern for the younger generation. I smiled when I heard all this as I recognized our similarities. Ever since, I've felt his warrior blood in my veins and have tried to honor his memory as I walk through life.

After my father died, my mother struggled, living in Argentina with two small children. Our family immigrated to America, but my brother and I were often sent back to live with relatives in Argentina when mom was working and unable to care for us. The separations were difficult, and our childhood left lasting scars. Then, during my summer visit to Miami when I was 16 years old, everything changed.

TAKEOFF

My mother had been a teacher in Argentina but wasn't credentialed in the U.S., so she worked as a traffic and operations agent for TACA Airlines at the Miami International Airport (MIA). Going to work with her was my first exposure to aviation.

I had been planning to return to Argentina to take the entrance exam for admission to the Faculty of Medicine. Instead, I decided to get a summer job at Wardair Canada (which later became Canadian Airlines). I was fluent in French, which gave me an advantage. One of my tasks at Wardair during those pre-internet days was to retrieve the flight plans from the teletype machine and take them to the pilots. I remember my feeling of intrigue and admiration for the uniformed pilots and my attraction to the cockpit. I started to think I wanted to become a pilot.

But when I mentioned my intention to people around me, I was immediately discouraged. I would hear things like, "You're crazy!" and "You have no money." Or my favorite, "But you're a woman!" This kind of talk stirred my warrior blood. My mother neither encouraged nor discouraged me. So, I set out on a journey to find out more.

There were two flight training airports near us, and I visited the flight schools at both. I found I didn't have the means to enroll in a flight school, but I wasn't going to let a little thing like money stop me. I found it to be more economical to rent an airplane and hire a flight instructor to get my private pilot's license. I worked and saved for private instruction, all the way through my commercial pilot rating.

I met my future husband the day I received my private pilot's license. I remember waiting for the FAA flight examiner in the small lobby at Tursair, a flight school at Opa Locka airport. I was 17 years old, wearing a t-shirt with the words *Nice, Côte d'Azur*. Sitting nearby was a tall, handsome, flight instructor, who was looking at me, and then came over to talk. He introduced himself as Frederick and asked me if I was French. He told me he was Belgian, but that his mom lived near Nice. We chatted a few minutes until the examiner arrived. After my exam, Fred was the first to congratulate me and we exchanged phone numbers.

Our friendship was incentive for me to find a job next door, at Hangar One, a fixed base operator. We began our courtship when I was 18 and he was 29. When we announced our intention to marry the following year, many people scoffed and predicted the marriage would last six months. It's been thirty-nine years and counting!

Throughout my career, I have not faced much discrimination being a woman, but my biggest challenge came early on. My friend Charlie and I were both hired at a commuter airline called Air New Orleans. We were trained, and then immediately furloughed when financing for new airplanes fell through. Charlie and another pilot in the class found work at an airline called Southern Air Transport. However, the operation did not have any women pilots and I found out they had no plans to hire any. Again, my warrior spirit began to stir. I was ready for the fight.

Southern Air's office was just a small trailer in the northwest corner of MIA. When I didn't hear back after sending in my resume, I called and was able to reach the secretary for the Director of Operations. She just happened to be Latina.

"I know you're hiring pilots because you hired my friend Charlie," I said to her. "I have the same qualifications he does, and I'd like to get an interview."

"They're not hiring women," she answered, honestly.

"Well, tell them if they don't see me, I'm going to come down to your office and sit on your doorstep until I get an interview," I said. I meant it too, but a couple of days after that conversation, I was called for an interview. To this day, I remember the feeling of elation when I was hired as a first officer on their civilian version of the Lockheed C-130.

People worried about me being the only woman pilot at the airline, but I fearlessly reported to the first day of class wearing a blue floral dress with a dainty lace collar. All eyes were on me as I sat down with a feminine, yet "don't mess with me" vibe that others recognized. Perhaps it explains why the men I work with routinely come to genuinely respect and appreciate me. They treat me like fathers and brothers, and I love them back for what I learn from them. I was the first woman hired at the company, but it was only the first of my "firsts" in aviation.

Pilots at Southern Air flew all over the world and were gone from home for long periods. The flying was challenging, and I thrive with challenges, but it was not conducive to family life or to raising children. My colleagues suggested I apply to the commercial airlines, and in 1988, after a four-phase interview process that took more than a year, I was hired at American Airlines. It was tough leaving Southern Air, who had given me the opportunity to be the youngest woman in the world to become a jet captain, at age 25, on a Southern Air Transport Boeing 707.

A year after I was hired at American, I was made supervisor of flying technical and flight engineer check airman at MIA. I supervised probationary flight engineers assigned to that new base, which opened after the purchase of routes from Eastern Airlines. I flew the B727 as flight engineer and first officer, the A300 and B767 and B777 as first officer, and then became the first Latina at American to be upgraded to captain, on an MD-80. I also became involved with the Allied Pilots Association (APA) and have served on several national committees over the years, including the communications committee. In early 2001, I became official spokesperson for the APA, just before the horror of 9/11 struck.

MEDIA AND MESSAGES

On September 11, I was living in California, getting my two children Patrick and Nathalie ready for school when the phone rang. It was a reporter from CNN en Español.

"Linda, have you seen what has happened?" she asked.

I turned on the TV and I couldn't believe my eyes as they showed the now iconic images of airliners flying into the World Trade Center towers.

"Do you have any comment?" I heard her say, as I tried to comprehend everything I was seeing and hearing.

"Not yet," I told her honestly, hanging up the phone.

I had received media training for my role as spokesperson, but nobody anticipated a scenario like this. During the next few weeks I made multiple appearances as APA spokesperson, representing the pilots of American Airlines. I held to the association's statements, without inserting my own opinions, which was a challenge at times.

Interviews revolved around security—questions about warnings, then issues like arming pilots. In the end, I learned how to operate under the pressure of media scrutiny and the importance of words, especially during live interviews when you cannot retract them. At one point, there was disagreement over whether I could speak for the labor side while wearing the airline uniform. In each skirmish, because labor and management both want the airline to succeed, common ground is sought and found.

After that, awards and honors came my way. I was chosen as one of the 100 Most Influential Latinas from both *Hispanic Business Magazine*, and *Hispanic Magazine*, and received a Tribute for Excellence in the Field of Transportation from Congress. Then, my life took another dramatic turn.

In 2004, I developed health issues which ultimately led to a loss of medical certification and a time on medical leave. Because I really thought I would never fly again, I considered options. An aviation law firm even offered to send me to law school, but I did not want to practice law. Instead, I completed a master's degree in education and started on a doctoral program in health education. The title of my dissertation was "Job Stress in Airline Pilots," and it explored our resilience as human beings. My work included researching meditative practices, and other holistic ways of handling stress. Then my son Patrick suffered a brain injury in 2010, and I withdrew from the program to concentrate on his care.

About that time, I also had a column in the Orange County Register called "From the Cockpit." I pitched the idea to the editor after fielding many questions from friends and family. It was nice visibility for me, twice a month, and kept me connected to aviation.

FOREVER LEARNING

After Patrick was better, I recovered my medical certification to fly and returned to American Airlines, where my graduate degree allowed me to pursue opportunities in the flight training department. I have been a check airman on the A320, and currently am on the B787. I fly routes to Asia, Europe, and South America and instruct and evaluate pilots in simulators at our Flight Academy in Dallas Fort Worth (DFW). I'm again involved with the union, serving on the training committee, and sometimes posting poetry on a "Morning Haiku" thread in our internal forum. It allows even the most competitive pilots to get in touch with their sensitive side.

My grit and warrior blood have helped me through the hard times in my aviation career, and I hope today's young people also find that sense of determination and perseverance as they face the distractions and challenges of modern society. It's also important they evaluate the significance of their decisions, for it is our youth who will carve our path into the future.

I'd like to think that if my grandfather were alive, he would be proud of his granddaughter. Even though I can't thank him personally, I can certainly honor him by continuing to carry his warrior spirit into everything I do.

Linda Pfeiffer Pauwels is a Boeing 787 Captain and Check Airman at American Airlines. She can be reached at pfeiffer.pauwels@ gmail.com.

COVID-19 POSTSCRIPT

It's a hard time for the airlines, but beyond the effect COVID-19 has had on the industry, I marvel at how it has forced us into adaptability, resilience, and steadfastness.

Within my own immediate family, we've had to reassess our priorities. After making a recovery, my son Patrick went on to college, playing basketball for the University of Maine at Fort Kent, and graduating with a degree in behavioral science this May. Even though the winters are harsh in northern Maine, he decided to remain there where he found an internship with good job prospects. This would not have happened without COVID-19.

My daughter Nathalie, who is a graduate of the U.S. Naval Academy, is close to getting her commercial pilot's license in American Airlines' cadet academy. However, with the industry in turmoil from COVID-19, she may need to tap into her other abilities to find secure employment, or alternatively, attend graduate school.

Even though we moved to DFW, and my husband Fred could be enjoying retirement, he has decided to stay on as a contract instructor for Boeing in Miami during these uncertain times.

As for me, I continue to keep my horizons open, and look for opportunities to use the unique skills I have been fortunate to acquire. It's the secret to staying young at heart!

JET SET TECHNICIAN

SANDRA GRANADOS

CURRENT POSITION
BBJ Lead Flight Technician, Gary Jet Center

FAVORITE AIRCRAFT
Boeing 747- It is and will always be the "queen of the skies" and my forever "wow!"

FAVORITE QUOTE
"Don't ever negate your gift. Embrace it, nourish it, strengthen it, and share it."

FUN FACT
I recently visited my seventy-third country.

Prior to the COVID-19 pandemic impact on air travel, many days of the month you would find me comfortably riding a beautiful, Boeing 737 corporate jet known as a BBJ (Boeing Business Jet), or a Bombardier Challenger 650, to amazing destinations around the world like historic Europe, the exotic Middle East, and picturesque China and Japan. Imagine an aircraft that looks like a flying office, with all the luxury you'd expect from a corporate jet, like plush leather reclining seats and beautiful gleaming wood trim, several bedrooms, bathrooms with showers, a conference/dining room and full kitchen. Sometimes, we would visit several countries a day. Aboard, the team had access to seamless and high-speed internet, and everything was always in tip top condition. I know that to be true, because I'm the one who kept it that way!

I never expected that my training as an Airframe & Powerplant mechanic would lead me to a life of globe-trotting at Boeing, yet as the lead flight technician for the company through the Gary Jet Center in Indiana, it's part of the job. And it's amazing to think that for years, the career so suited to me wasn't even on my radar!

FLIGHT AND FANCY

Growing up in the Bucktown neighborhood of Chicago, and I guess you could say I was a tomboy. There are four children in my family, but I spent most of my time with my brother, who was only a year older than I. We enjoyed the same things, but one thing we loved was racing remote control cars. Whenever we crashed, I reveled in the opportunity to take the car apart and get to the bottom of how it worked. Fixing things came naturally to me.

My dad was a typical macho man from Mexico, with a

deep-rooted machismo attitude, who believed his wife should be in the kitchen. But he was proud of my ability to fix things and would include me in his projects for his real estate ventures. While most kids spent their Saturday mornings watching cartoons, I was up bright and early to help my dad pull up carpet, paint walls, change sinks and install flooring. He was a patient teacher. "If your brother and I can do this, you can too, and you will thank me when you are older" he would tell me.

I learned about aviation during our family trips, where we would fly to Guadalajara, Mexico every year to visit my grandparents. My mom loves to travel and says she now lives vicariously through me, since she hasn't visited many places. However, she took us on road trips to experience history and different cultures, and she ignited my curiosity about one day exploring the rest of the world. As this emerging interest and my affection for air travel began to meld, I started thinking about becoming a pilot.

However, at my smaller, Catholic private high school's college fair, there were never any representatives from aviation in attendance. When I approached my guidance counselor and requested more information, she looked at me in shock and told me nobody had ever asked before, and that we would just have to do the research together.

After considering larger, public school flight programs, we settled upon Lewis University in nearby Romeoville, Illinois because I was comfortable with the smaller enrollment and class sizes there. I started the school's flight program, but my progress was slow and constantly delayed by the weather, the flight instructor, or my schedule. So, I continued my training at General Aviators, a flight school out of Midway Airport, during one complete summer until I earned my private pilot's license.

Getting my commercial license was the next step but affording flight school and college tuition simultaneously was overwhelming. The military option wasn't right for me at the time. I could not give up though, as I knew then that the passion for Aviation had already been impressed upon my heart.

Then, one day, I was in one of the aviation buildings when a Lewis professor stopped me in the hall to talk. She was a retired airline A&P (airframe and powerplant) mechanic from United Airlines.

"I've seen you around," she said, undoubtedly noticing me as one of the few females in the building. "What program are you in?"

I told her about my desire to fly, the difficult journey, and my financial challenges.

"Have you ever thought about a career in aviation maintenance?" she asked me.

I felt like a deer in the headlights, frozen in amazement. Of course! Why had I never thought of it before? It was the perfect combination of my skills and aviation!

I finished my sophomore year as a transfer into the aviation maintenance program. Then in my junior year, I attended a college fair filled with aviation representatives, including one from ATA (American Trans Air) Airlines. I asked them how to apply in the future and to my surprise, they asked me to come in and interview, even though I was still in school. The HR representative told me they would work around my schedule and help me finish my senior year of college. For them, that meant putting me on the night shift from ten o'clock at night until six-thirty in the morning. I took the job.

For the next year, I would rush home, shower, do some homework and get about 4-5 hrs of sleep until I had to go to work and then do it all over again the next day. Looking back, it was an insane schedule, but it prepared me for the crazy jet lag and sleep schedule I would be facing in my future role with Boeing!

The first time I walked into the hangar bay to report to work at ATA, I hadn't yet received my uniform, so I was dressed in street clothes. The big, burly men all turned to look at me.

"Did you come to work with your dad today?" one of them asked me in all seriousness.

We all laughed when I told them who I was. Their surprise and response was expected, as I later found out I was the only female mechanic at our midway station and the first Latina female mechanic to get hired at ATA. I was 19 years old at the time and knew that I had to prove myself. They soon learned that I was one woman who wasn't afraid to get her hands dirty.

I was up for doing anything the men were. That included riding the lift forty feet up in the air to replace components on the top of the vertical fin or working in extreme weather conditions during Chicago's gruesome winters. I recall having to change an engine valve during a polar vortex. The wind chill was -25F and my coworker and I had to alternate working on it minutes at a time without our gloves on to avoid getting frostbite. I learned quickly that I had to adapt and overcome the many challenges that I would face during my employment with ATA.

My crazy schedule made for a tough senior year but as an entry-level mechanic the excitement of seeing those heavy jet airplanes in the hangar never got old. Despite the mental pressure and lack of social life, I was glad I accepted their offer when I did. I was hired in May of 2000, and the next year 9/11 happened. Many of my fellow classmates had difficulty finding a job after graduation in the temporarily paralyzed industry. By this time, I had already accrued enough seniority to endure the layoffs that began as a result of the lingering effects of 9/11.

In 2006, ATA declared bankruptcy and I started looking for a new position. The solid foundation and experience that I had cemented in those 6 years of employment, made me a very qualified candidate for my next endeavor. I was completely thrilled when I applied and got the job at Gary Jet Center.

LIFE OF A FLIGHT TECHNICIAN

You may wonder what a flight technician is doing aboard a corporate jet during a flight mission. I am in charge of the aircraft's overall Airworthiness status. I address any mechanical issues experienced during flight or on the ground. I prepare the airplane for departure, ensuring we have an accurate fuel load and making sure all mechanical systems are working properly.

When a corporate jet flew overseas as regularly as it did for Boeing in the pre-COVID-19 era, it made logistical sense for a technician to be onboard. All routine or emergency maintenance must be signed off in the logbook by an FAA-approved A&P technician. In foreign countries, it's not always easy to find someone who can legally do it nor has the experience to work on such a complex custom jet.

I would not fly on the corporate jet all the time, but instead would take a commercial flight a day prior to meeting our airplane at the first foreign destination. Since I am technically "on the clock" when I fly on the corporate jet, I have to plan accordingly to not exceed the allowable 14-hour duty day. I need to be fresh and ready to work 14 hours if the airplane arrives with a mechanical issue. Arriving a day ahead of the airplane allows me to overcome the jetlag that comes with crossing multiple time zones and be ready to work! Then, I typically board the corporate jet and finish out the rest of the itinerary.

Performing duties in a foreign country can be challenging. Some of these challenges include finding replacement parts for the aircraft while dealing with the various cultural differences and language barriers. When I visit Saudi Arabia, for example, I must wear the required hijab and traditional garb. The Saudi men will not take direction from any woman, including me. I must have one of our male crew members standing by to help communicate and give instructions to the Saudi men on my behalf.

We have a group of about forty pilots and twenty flight attendants that I see on rotation. After a flight, we have a huddle and I collect information from the pilots on any mechanical problems they experience. I also address any onboard problems such as internet connectivity or any additional issues reported by our flight attendants. Every trip is different in the sense that we can have a maintenance-free flight or one where numerous maintenance issues arise.

Sometimes there is time to tour our incredible destinations and explore the different cultures. This is what I love most about my job. There are certain places that I will never get tired of visiting, such as the Great Wall of China. The feeling I get when I stand on such a grandiose structure that extends for miles beyond the horizon is awe-inspiring.

MISSION TO CHINA

In February 2020, when COVID-19 was beginning to emerge, I had just returned from a major trip through China. We were just starting to hear about the virus, but I was tested for safety. It was negative, and I have been tested three times since with the same result. These days, the flights have been drastically reduced and the ones that take place are a logistical nightmare between country restrictions, quarantine requirements, and the difficulty of getting documents and visas from consulate offices that are closed here in the U.S.

I was happy and proud, however, to have taken part in an amazing airlift mission to bring back PPE from China. Boeing donated the transportation means to retrieve more than 500,000 facemasks and pieces of PPE that was designated for the state of

New Hampshire. I volunteered for the mission, in part because quarantining would be absolutely required afterwards, that process would be a lot easier for me as opposed to my co-workers that have families.

Our planes are not equipped for cargo, so it was challenging figuring out how to fit and safely store hundreds of two-foot by three-foot boxes in our passenger cabin. We put them everywhere we could--on the beds, in the bathrooms, and stacked to the aircraft ceiling. I was in charge of securing them for the flight home, without the common anchor points normally available on a cargo aircraft. It took planning and creativity to do it right!

Our team of five left Gary on April 15 and spent the night in Anchorage, Alaska. We continued another nine hours to Shanghai, where our cargo was. The Chinese were ready for us, with their conveyor belts and loading equipment ready to go as we taxied in. We had a limited amount of time because all flights were required to land and depart in the same day. We worked quickly and completed the load in under three hours. Then we flew to nearby Seoul and spent the night. We arrived in Manchester, New Hampshire on April 18, to the cheers and greetings of residents, politicians, and those who sponsored and made the mission possible. The trip took 13,566 miles and almost thirty-five flight hours, but the biggest measurement I felt was my pride in being part of the Boeing team that made it possible.

It was also my work with Boeing that led me to receive the Aviation Pros AMT 40 Under 40 Next Gen Award. I was on a beach in Italy when I got the call informing me that I was one of the recipients of the award. I remember looking out over the Mediterranean, reflecting on my career and what a wonderful ride it has been. I had recently checked off my 73rd country! All because a professor stopped me in the hall one day and introduced me to this fascinating world of aircraft maintenance.

It's so clear that young people need that mentorship and contact with those who can guide and encourage them. Very few things rival seeing an airplane up close and sitting in the cockpit touching the controls. The excitement, interest, and curiosity this experience creates is unparalleled. I always answer the call to attend college fairs or gatherings where I can tell others about what I do and for those of us in aviation, it is our responsibility to do it too.

Continuing to provide that exposure, I am confident that more kids, and especially more girls, will decide to follow a career in this exciting industry full of boundless opportunities. Perhaps one day I will be someone's lighted path, just like Mrs. Maddock was for me.

It's a great career that makes for an exciting life, but above all... nothing compares to working above the clouds!

Sandra Granados is lead BBJ Flight technician at Gary Jet Center supporting Boeing. She can be reached at Sandra.granados@ boeing.com.

COVID-19 POSTSCRIPT

Even though so many trips have been cancelled and our fleet of aircraft isn't flying as often anymore because of COVID-19, there is still plenty to be done. Aircraft need a lot of maintenance, even when they are grounded. To stay current, pilots' cycle through and fly the aircraft every seven days, which creates the need for inspection and maintenance. I'm not used to being grounded, but I've recently purchased a house, and that has been keeping me very busy. My biggest project has been building an outdoor fireplace in the backyard, which required running a gas line from the house to the structure. I impressed myself with the final product!

I'm looking forward to the days I'm back to my normal routine, but for now I'm staying busy and trying to enjoy the temporary change of pace.

FROM FEAR TO FLIGHT

JEANNETTE COLLAZO

CURRENT POSITION

Aspiring aviator & President of Lurdez Consulting Group, Inc.

FAVORITE AIRCRAFT

Remos GX

It's the plane that helped me love aviation.

FAVORITE QUOTE

God, grant me the serenity to accept the things I cannot change,
courage to change the things I can, and wisdom to know the
difference " -Reinhold Niebuhr

FUN FACT

I'm a study in opposites—I love kickboxing and meditation.

A beloved former President of the United States once told us, "You have nothing to fear but fear itself." In the case of aviation, that's very true, at least in my experience. Fear has been my biggest obstacle to overcome in my flight training, and although it tried it's hardest to keep me grounded, I eventually rose above it.

My journey to becoming a pilot started in a sleek, white sport plane piloted by my friend and fellow aviation enthusiast, Jackie Camacho-Ruiz. She had invited me out for a flight. I had no misgivings whatsoever. But on my way to the airport, she called me and told me that the flight had been cancelled because the plane needed maintenance.

"You've got a raincheck, Jeannette, don't worry," she said.

A few weeks later, I was at an anniversary party for Jackie's marketing company, JJR Marketing. She was giving away prizes, including a flight with her, to the person who guessed the number of times she had successfully completed a takeoff and landing. Guess who won? I couldn't help but think that this fortunate coincidence was a sign that taking a flight was something I really needed to do.

DISCOVERIES AND REVELATIONS

The day of our flight was a beautiful, Friday evening in September. The weather was so nice, Jackie even took the doors off the little sport plane. Then, as the little plane roared down the runway and lifted us into the air, I was overcome with a feeling of exhilaration. As I saw the earth below become a patchwork quilt of landscape, I felt an unexplainable, strange feeling. It was as if the altitude had touched my soul and was beckoning me to become one with it.

I was intrigued, and a bit amused at my feelings. Me? Become a pilot? What had put that idea into my head? I figured the feeling would pass, and I didn't have to worry about it that day. We landed at a nearby airport and over happy hour drinks and appetizers, we got a little personal. I confided to Jackie that I had just ended a relationship of about a year because of long distance.

"Well, if you became a pilot, you could cut that commute in half," she said with a twinkle in her eye. She was joking. But was it a joke?

On the way home we were treated to the glorious view of a sunset from three thousand feet. As I watched the beautiful amber glow descend behind the horizon, I decided to tell Jackie one more secret.

"You know what?" I said to her. "I think I'm going to do this. I think I'm going to learn to fly."

"What??" Jackie replied, incredulously.

"Yeah," I said, surrendering to that mysterious pull that I was feeling once more. "I'm going to become a pilot."

FACING FEAR

Being in a plane with Jackie was one thing. Going up for a discovery flight with a flight instructor who expected you to take the controls on your first time up, was quite another.

Hoping to replicate the exciting feeling I had with Jackie, I arranged a discovery flight with the owner of a small aviation company called Simply Fly in Aurora, Illinois. He told me right away that we would be switching seats during the flight, but he would handle take offs and landings. He gave me a broken off broomstick as a pretend instrument to teach me how to control the altitude of the plane prior to getting on it. The mere thought of it all started to make my heart pound faster. Was it excitement? No, I realized. It was fear.

When we got up in the air, I was even more afraid. Every little jerk of the plane turned my knuckles white. This wasn't the feeling I wanted to have; why was I so scared?

It wasn't the altitude, I realized. It was the lack of control. And of being able to be in control.

When it was my turn to fly the plane, I gripped the controls, just as I had done with the broomstick during my ground lesson. But this time, my hands were shaking, almost uncontrollably. I knew the instructor wasn't going to let anything happen, but I was still freaking out. All sorts of fearful thoughts ran through my mind. What if the instructor had a heart attack in mid-air? How would I ever land the plane? How could I become a pilot if I was afraid when I was at the controls and also afraid when I wasn't at the controls because then, I really wasn't in control!

When we were safely back on the ground, I recognized that my magical feeling had somehow morphed into an interesting combination of fear and desire to gain control and conquer that fear. I couldn't become a pilot if I couldn't control my fear. If Jackie was like an angel on my shoulder, delivering the message that I should become a pilot, my fear was a devil sitting on my other shoulder, telling me to give up.

But my feelings about flying were not unlike my feelings about my life and career. I feel in control of them now, but it wasn't always that way. At times I have faced daunting challenges as an IT project manager, whether it was a particularly difficult assignment, or a conflict with someone on my team. In my life I've had to make tough decisions and overcome the adversity of life-threatening asthma in my childhood. It took time, faith, perseverance, and experience to overcome my fear in life and work, but I was always able to do it. I decided if I could conquer my fears there, I could conquer them in the cockpit of a sports plane too.

I searched myself and realized that deep down the urge that I had felt to learn to fly had never left after all. So, I began my flight training, and through repetition, my instructors slowly desensitized me to all the things I feared. During one lesson, Jack kept telling me how we were going to learn how to manage a stalled engine in mid-air. The very idea was so frightening that I completely forgot my usual fear when I was taking off.

When it was time to stall the plane, the butterflies in my stomach returned. Multi-tasking between the radio, navigating, and maintaining the right altitude was a lot to handle at one time. Yet, I was successful, and if people asked me if I had a good time that day, I would definitely have said yes.

DECIDING TO BE FEARLESS

Fear was my biggest obstacle, but it slowly melted away with the heat of my desire to become a pilot coupled with Jack's crafty instruction techniques. The next biggest obstacle was the volatile Chicago weather. It was hard to find nice days to practice, let alone solo. They told me I was ready to solo in October of 2019. I finally agreed with them in November. Then, a series of life events, coupled with bad weather, and then a pandemic, kept me from actually scheduling a solo run. It looked like I was on hold for a while.

When the state of Illinois went on lockdown from COVID-19, I did everything I was supposed to do in order to protect myself. I worked remotely with my clients and stayed home. Because of my asthmatic condition, I had a compromised immune system and my doctor advised me not to go out at all. I even had all my groceries and supplies delivered. But I couldn't stop thinking about flying.

In late April, on a whim, I called the flight school and asked if they were seeing anybody for solo flights. They were! Now I was torn between my doctor's orders and my desire to complete this important step in my training.

On May 5, the day before my tentative solo date, something happened that changed my attitude about everything. I was home alone and getting something out of my closet. I was reaching up and pulling out a bag off the top shelf when I accidentally bumped my nebulizer, which I use to treat my asthma. The eight-pound machine came tumbling off the shelf at breakneck speed and landed on my head so solidly I thought I was going to pass out. My head throbbed and I felt like my skull was going to come off. I made it to the freezer and put an ice pack on my head. For the next ten minutes, I had a splitting headache.

When I felt a little better, I called the doctor. He had me check my symptoms and was certain I didn't need to go to the doctor, but needed rest, at least for 24 hours.

As I lay on the couch holding the ice pack, I had a realization. Here I was, in my house, trying to protect myself from a virus and this machine could have killed me. I decided then I wouldn't live my life in fear. I would rather take my chances outside in the world, doing what I love, than die in my own home from a freak accident.

The next morning, I awoke feeling much better and with a renewed spirit and beautiful energy running through me. "Today is the day!" I thought.

I checked the schedule and both of my instructors' calendars were wide open, which was a huge surprise to me because they are always booked. I then had to decide which one was the instructor with whom I would do my solo. I decided to do it with Jack, since he was the instructor who had gotten me past so many of my fears. Like he would say: He desensitized me! He had once told me; he had never seen someone so scared of flying actually make it all the way to solo. I was determined. And I was ready.

It was a beautiful day, about fifty degrees and not too windy. Jack took me to the airport in nearby Hinkley, which had a grass, rather than cement runway. That threw me at first, but I took several practice loops before it was my turn to go it alone.

Then I was in the cockpit, with just me, special stones to give me energy and an angel and saint medal to keep watch over me. I had a beautiful take off and circled around three times until the approach and everything was right for landing. I descended smoothly and methodically, getting closer and closer to the mossy runway, until suddenly, I was back on the ground, safe and sound. I DID IT!

I have a Facebook video of me leaping out of the plane and jumping for joy. I was out of my mind with excitement. Jack rejoiced with me. He was so proud.

And now I must continue the journey. I am an entrepreneur and do not plan to pursue a career as a pilot, but I feel like becoming a pilot has a very important purpose in my life which has yet to be revealed to me. I feel I have been guided down this path, despite my fear, so I'm sure there is a meaningful purpose behind it all.

I'm a dog lover and I saw a poster for volunteer pilots to help transport dogs in need of rescue. Maybe that's my aviation future.

I can't golf but now I can take clients on airplane trips. Maybe that's in my aviation future.

So many young girls don't realize how wonderful aviation is. Maybe exposing them to aviation and serving as a mentor pilot is in my future.

Whatever comes my way, I know that aviation has made me a more fearless and faithful person. And that's a skill that translates to my personal and professional life too.

Jeannette Collazo is a motivational speaker, aviator, and President of Lurdez Consulting Group, an IT project management firm. She can be reached at jeannettecollazo.com.

COVID-19 POSTSCRIPT

I have been fortunate that COVID-19 has impacted me more positively than negatively. I'm lucky to have a job that I can do from home, and I've done essential work helping companies transition their employees to working from home. I've had more time to spend with my dog and my family. I've been able to call my mom every day and hone in on the things that matter most in life.

I've developed an even greater appreciation of our earth and have started to recycle more regularly. The quarantine has also helped me take time to think of others and pray for them. At the end of this all, when we finally see each other in person for work and play, I know we will emerge as people with a better understanding of what really matters in life.

ABOUT THE AUTHOR

JACQUELINE S. RUIZ

Jackie is a visionary social entrepreneur that has created an enterprise of inspiration. Her keen sense of service coupled with the vision to bring good to the world have led her to create two successful award-winning companies, establish two nonprofit organizations, publish 17 books, create many  products, and has held dozens of events around the world in just the past decade.

She is often referred to as a "dream catcher" as her strategies have supported thousands of women, authors and young ladies to live a life of significance. Jacqueline's quest to be a servant leader extends to every area of her life. She has shared her inspiration in four continents and aligned with some of the most powerful brands to elevate others. At only 37 years of age, she has achieved what most would not do in an entire lifetime. Being a cancer survivor sparked a sense of urgency to serve and transcend.

Jacqueline believes that magix (yes, a made-up word that means magic x 10) is the interception of profit and impact.

"Taking off is optional, landing on your dreams is mandatory."

-Jacqueline S. Ruiz

Made in the USA
Middletown, DE
10 May 2021

39378650R10120